# {Quick & Kosher} MEALS IN MINUTES

FROM THE BRIDE WHO KNEW NOTHING

## Jamie Geller

FELDHEIM PUBLISHERS
JERUSALEM     NEW YORK

# {Quick & Kosher} MEALS IN MINUTES

### FROM THE BRIDE WHO KNEW NOTHING

## Jamie Geller

Art Director
Devorah Rosen Goldman

Graphic Design
Julie Farkas

Photography
Ann Stratton
Assistants
Tanya Salazar
Brian Tamborello
Jonathan Schultz

Food Styling
Carrie Purcell
Assistant
Sarah Abrams

Prop Styling
Pamela Duncan Silver
Assistant
Paola Ramirez

Content Editor/Writer
Charlotte Friedland

Recipe Development
Laurie Knoop
Paige McCurdy-Flynn

Recipe Testing
Laurie Knoop
Paige McCurdy-Flynn
Ginna Mungiovi
Donna Fields
Malke Freifeld
Jerry Grunn
Richard Grunn

Recipe Editing
Sheilah Kaufman
Paula Jacobson

Wine Recommendations
Gary Landsman

Proofreading
Debra Wells
Sheilah Kaufman
Paula Jacobson
Carol Winer

Food Courtesy
Kosher.com

Publisher
Feldheim Publishers

Additional Photography
pages 34, 36, 38, 42, 44, 56, 60, 62, 98, 100,
102, 110, 112, 120, 124, 126, 130, 134, 146,
150, 152, 160, 162, 164, 186, 188, 202
Photography
Jerry Errico
Food Styling
Brian Preston-Campbell
Prop Styling
Dawn Sinkowski

## FELDHEIM PUBLISHERS
### JERUSALEM · NEW YORK

Feldheim Publishers
Jerusalem-New York
©2010 by Feldheim Publishers and Jamie Geller
Photographs ©2010 by Ann Stratton and Jerry Errico

Feldheim Publishers
POB 43163, Jerusalem, Israel 91431
208 Airport Executive Park, Nanuet, NY 10954
www.feldheim.com
www.kosher.com

ISBN 978-1-59826-596-5

Printed in China

This book is dedicated to my family,
the loves and lights of my life

Bracha Miriam, Rochel Naami,
Yaakov Leib Yosef, Avraham Yitzchak
and Nachum

For teaching this bride
everything she knows.

# {What's Inside}

{20} minute meals

{40} minute meals

{60} minute meals

{holiday} meals

# { Confessions of a Jewish Bride } FIVE YEARS LATER

unless you join the circus,
nobody teaches you how to juggle

In my first *Quick & Kosher* cookbook, I openly admitted that I got married

without a clue about anything in the kitchen. I could flip the lights on and

off, of course, but that was all. No way could I figure out what to do with

all those gadgets people gave me at my bridal shower. That book was a

painfully honest chronicle of how "the bride who knew nothing" learned

to food shop, plan, and cook meals in record time—and serve them confidently

to unsuspecting guests!

I discovered that learning how to cook is like learning anything else: you go to a class, pick

up a cookbook, watch a cooking show, ask a friend. But now—five years down the line—

with bedrooms filled with toy trucks and teddy bears, I find that I'm a beginner once again!

Nobody prepared me for what it's like to smell your dinner going up in smoke while you're

on your hands and knees behind the crib searching for a lost pacifier. Most cookbooks are

oblivious to the fact that your husband's boss (or worse, your picky sister-in-law) is coming

for dinner in an hour and you've got to magically cook up something impressive, despite the

fact that three kids are clutching your skirt, scraps of lunch are still on the table and chocolate

syrup is dripping from the counter onto the floor.

nobody prepared me for what it's like to smell
your dinner going up in smoke while you're on your hands
and knees behind the crib searching for a lost pacifier.

I'll level with you. I think the way to cook with kids around is "as fast as you can." And that's

why I've written this book. You need ideas and you need them quick. You've got to get it all

together and you're supposed to look terrific too. I can't help you with looking terrific—see

your cosmetician about that. But I can help you look calm, because I'm going to show you

how to get it all done in a flash. When you keep your cool, you look great.

Believe me, I know the value of this kind of help because I never got any. I won't pretend

to know all of your challenges—after all, I've never shuffled a mile in your slippers—and I

don't claim to have all the answers.

{ In fact, I'll confess that I'm not a real "chef," even though I play one on TV. Moreover, I still make mistakes in my own kitchen and everywhere else. Listen, the fact that I've written a cookbook doesn't make me immune to fiascos. Take a little episode in my life I'll call Hubby's Birthday Surprise.

As a loving and thoughtful wife, I decided to make my husband a birthday cake. The trouble was that it didn't occur to me until after he left for *minyan* the morning of his birthday. But I tried to think it through. It would take about 50 minutes for him to *daven*. Add a half hour for him to do his Sunday errands and yes! I can do it!

Just a few days before, he had been reminiscing about the terrific "snowman cake" his grandmother always baked for his birthday parties. Just talking about it put such a happy, boyish grin on his face that I resolved to recreate that cake. How hard could it be? Chalk up my zeal to hormones: I was just a few weeks from the "due date" of my son's birth day and I was feeling super-motherly.

It is a rainy morning, too close to 7:00 o'clock. I load my sleepy toddlers into the minivan and we tootle over to the supermarket. We race through the aisles looking for the essential ingredients, at least the ones I can remember. After three clerks and a manager tell me they don't stock specialty items like snowman cake molds, I strap the kids back into the car and dash home.

Back in the house, I decide to improvise the snowman using circular challah pans. I whip up the batter, pour it into the pans, and throw them in the oven. I change the kids out of their pajamas, feed them breakfast, and smell the cakes burning. I call that done. The canned white icing I bought covers only half of this singed, drooping, twenty-pound monster, so I make some chocolate cupcake frosting and slap it all over the rest. It already looks terrible—what can I lose? So I give the kids sprinkles, chocolate chips, Twizzlers, and potato chips; and they throw the stuff all over the cake with wild abandon.

I manage to lug the Snowthing to the table just as hubby walks in the door. The kids are giggling and jumping up and down. I'm covered with sweat and flour, but I try to smile as we lead him to our masterpiece. Singing "Happy Birthday" in our party hats, we watch *Abba* try to figure out what the monstrosity on the table is supposed to be. "It's a snowman cake, *Abba*, just like Great-grandma used to make!" they shout. Birthday Boy gives me a quizzical look then manfully takes a cake server in hand. Next, he tries a chef's knife (another option would be a chainsaw) to hack through the hard, crusty shell of the cake. The batter inside oozes out, totally raw, onto the table! He doesn't even take a lick of the icing. Instead, he runs for his camera. Staring after him, my eyes are a bit teary. And that's when my daughter climbs on my lap and whispers, "I told you, Mommy, we should have bought a cake from the bakery." }

Sound familiar? Through careful scientific research (ok—from swapping tales on the supermarket checkout line), I've ascertained that most of us have our share of kitchen horror stories and the stats seem to go up when there are children around.

I'm fairly new to the mommy biz. Though it seems like an endless job, in my better moments I realize that I am creating memories for my children. Even with my hectic career, I still dream about my kids looking back on their childhoods with images of Mommy being there at all the right moments, leading them on madcap outings and showing them how to bake brownies. It's all about love. Ok, since we're Jewish, love *and* food. My grandparents used to create the yummiest meals with such love that the aroma alone embraced you like a big hug. I always wanted a warm, homey kitchen like theirs.

even with my hectic career, I still dream about my kids looking back on their childhoods with images of Mommy being there at all the right moments, leading them on madcap outings and showing them how to bake brownies. It's all about love.

But then reality hit me. Don't get me wrong. My kids are wonderful, but during my single years, I never dreamed I'd spend most of my waking hours driving carpools in a minivan, or that I'd fish in my pocketbook for my BlackBerry and wind up sorting through baby wipes and half-chewed pretzels.

I learned to get a grip and figured out how to cook with kids around, how to cook for kids, make mealtimes fun (or at least tolerable), and stay focused on the things that count. And now I'm ready to pass my experience along to other frazzled moms and dads who, like me, are looking for some down-to-earth ideas for how to turn your kitchen into a fast-(delicious)-food joint.

So here comes another confession: I have learned that simple additions, flourishes, and clever combinations of ready-made foods can make a gourmet cook out of anyone, even me. It isn't magic: It's know-how.

Listen, we're all in this together. I know that some days you may have 60 minutes to spend preparing dinner, and other days you can barely squeeze out 20; so I've arranged this book corresponding to how much time *you* can spare. We're talking about full meals in just minutes, people.

To make the job even simpler, I put the recipes into complete menus so you don't have to waste time figuring out what goes with what. And even if you are accustomed to cooking a zillion hours for *Shabbos* and *Yom Tov*, I can show you how to cut your prep time way down in my chapter on preparing for the holidays—or any special day.

## How easy is that?

# {The Total Mommy Kitchen} A MAGNET OF LOVE

make your home, and especially the kitchen,
a place to forge memories

If you're anything like me, you finished off your *Sheva Brachos* week with plans for intimate candlelight dinners with your spouse—complete with lace tablecloths and crystal stemware—the works. And again, if your life is anything like mine, those visions dimmed pretty quickly as you found yourself scraping hardened oatmeal off the baby's highchair. I'm not saying we *never* indulged in those romantic dinners. We did *so*—um, I think on our first anniversary. Not sure.

In any case, now that we're all grown up, we've discovered that to live happily ever after means sweating the small stuff in every sphere of life as a spouse, homemaker, and parent —even if you also happen to be a business exec with heavy deadlines and a heavier boss. You're working hard on every front—bringing home a paycheck, making meals, soothing fevered children, picking up toys from the floor and shirts from the cleaners. That's what they really meant at your wedding when they blessed you to build a *"bayis ne'eman b'Yisrael"* —a home faithful to Jewish ideals. You thought it was going to be inspiration at the *Shabbos* table, teaching your kids *Torah*, making special treats for the holidays—and it is. But it's also the daily grind of packing lunches and figuring out how to make spinach look appetizing.

You find that you don't go out to eat as often as you used to and you are entertaining more and more at home. And sometimes you're hosting a crowd that's all under five years old. It goes with the territory.

I'm going to teach you how to enjoy it. You will see that you can make your home, and especially its epicenter called "the kitchen," a magnet of love and a place to forge memories you and your family will treasure. In the following sections, you will find the tips and strategies that can make it all happen. We'll fill in *Your Tool Box* and discuss how to *Create a Comfort Zone*.

Welcome to the wonderful challenge of creating the
Total Mommy* Kitchen!

# {Your Tool Box}

If you put me on a desert island with a primitive kitchen and tell me I can have 10 things to make my life easier, my first question would be, "can I have one more?" Who wrote the "Top 10" rule? Let's think out of the box, people, and start a Top 11 trend! That's because after setting up my kitchen with the basics (a knife set, cookware, phone number of the nearest take-out) there are 11 specialty items in my kitchen that not only increase efficiency, they are the magic tools that make a so-so meal into a knock-your-socks-off feast! See how many of these you already have in your kitchen; then go get the rest—and you won't be sorry.

### Food Processor
Ok—so I'm assuming that my desert island has electricity. I wrote about the amazing benefits of food processors in *Quick & Kosher Recipes From The Bride Who Knew Nothing*, but I am going to repeat myself here, just in case you have any doubts about splurging on one of these darling little machines. Food processors are indispensable time savers for jobs like puréeing, mincing, or shredding almost *anything*.

. . . . . . . . . . . . . . . . . . . . . . . . . . . . . . . . . . . . . . . . . . . . . . . . . . . . . . . . . . . . . . . . . .

### Grill Pans
Great for everything from burgers and steaks to grilled fish, veggies, and panini, heavy-bottomed, ovenproof grill pans are worth the price. Look for the kind with wide ridges (5/16" or more) because they enable a larger area of caramelization, resulting in richer flavor. It's a good idea to go for aluminum rather than cast iron, unless you want to combine cooking dinner with your weight-lifting workout. The aluminum pans are not only lighter to handle, they also leave nicer grill marks on your food. Though grill pans can be somewhat costly, a couple of grill pans are cheaper than two outdoor grills, and you can use them all year round, regardless of the weather.

### Mandoline

Once you get the hang of it, a mandoline saves time creating perfectly uniform vegetable and fruit slices and juliennes. I especially like to use it for apples, potatoes, cucumbers, and carrots. Because they have an adjustable blade, you can get varying thicknesses with much more speed and precision then you can with a knife. Be sure to follow instructions and use the supplied hand guard: mandoline blades are razor sharp.

### Microplane®

These precision graters originated in the woodshop as rasps (a coarse file with sharp, raised points). When the Microplane tool company started getting orders from chefs, a new product was born. They are perfect for many things, including cheese, ginger or nutmeg and for zesting citrus fruits.

### Ovenproof Skillets

One of the secret weapons used by restaurant chefs for turning out large quantities of food at the last minute is a good quality skillet that can withstand oven temperatures. Skillets should be heavy enough to conduct heat to the food evenly. You can use your skillet for excellent caramelization and crusting of your food on top of the stove and for cooking it through by finishing it in the oven.

### PepperMate®

Just the handiest pepper mill there is, and I wouldn't start cooking without it. I prefer this brand to your standard grinders because they're simple to refill, easy to work, and catch the ground pepper (or other spices) in a detachable cup. You can adjust the grind from fine to coarse, a valuable feature if you're picky like me. (Just between us, Paula Deen, Rachael Ray, and Ina Garten all say it's their fave, so you'll be in good company.)

### Potato Masher

When a full-blown purée is not what you are after, and you don't want your potatoes to turn gummy from overwork, a potato masher is what you need. Mashers come in all shapes and sizes, but the most common version has a zigzag pattern. They're terrific for making other things too, such as applesauce, hummus, even bagel-shop-style egg salad and tuna fish.

### Reamer or Juicer

Fresh lemon and lime juice add spark and vitality to food. Whether for cooking or baking, having a reamer on hand makes short work of getting all the juice out of citrus. (BTW, I do use the bottled version in a pinch.)

### Salad Spinner

Although pre-washed bag salad is one of G-d's great gifts to those of us who are pressed for time, this simple device dries salad greens and herbs with almost no effort. Washing and drying your own salad is much more affordable than buying the pre-washed bags. Look for a spinner that has a nonslip bottom and one-handed operation.

### Scissors

Good pairs of scissors (yes, you'll probably need more than one pair) are indispensable in the kitchen for everything from trimming meat to snipping herbs and opening packages. Poultry shears make it especially easy to cut through chickens, and can be used for a variety of other foods as well.

### Tongs

Like an extension of your hand, tongs may be the most useful and versatile kitchen tool you will ever buy. I recommend having a drawer full of tongs in all shapes and sizes. They come in especially handy when dealing with raw meat or piping hot foods. Extra-long tongs are a must when grilling, and shorter tongs are practical for serving at the table.

# { Bonus! A Slick Little Primer About Oils }

It's not a tool in the traditional sense (so I'm not including it in my Top 11 items), but every chef knows that selecting the right oil for each recipe is essential for cooking success. Here's a basic oil primer to put you in the know.

The first important tip is to know the relative smoking points of the oils in your pantry. The smoking point is the temperature at which the oil starts to break down and turn into a gas. For frying, you want oil with a high smoking point.

### every chef knows that selecting the right oil for each recipe is essential for cooking success

Some oils are also considered more "heart healthy" than others, primarily because they are high in monounsaturated and polyunsaturated fat and low in saturated fat. I've put a ♥ symbol next to these, but if you are concerned about fats and oils for health reasons, you should consult a nutritionist to find out which are best for you.

♥ Canola Oil
Excellent for sautéing and deep-frying, this vegetable oil has a very mild flavor and is good to use when you don't need or want an assertive flavor.

. . . . . . . . . . . . . . . . . . . . . . . . . . .

Corn Oil
The high smoking point of corn oil makes it appropriate for frying as well as general uses.

. . . . . . . . . . . . . . . . . . . . . . . . . . .

Cottonseed Oil
A lot of people use this oil on Passover in place of corn oil or other *kitniyos* products. While it has a mild taste and can be used in baking, cooking, and frying, be aware that it is one of the worst oils in terms of heart health. Many nutritionists deem it too high in saturated fat and too low in monounsaturated fat. Because cotton is not considered a food, farmers are legally permitted to use more and different pesticides than allowed on food crops, so it can contain pesticide residue. There are other kosher-for-Passover oils on the market.

. . . . . . . . . . . . . . . . . . . . . . . . . . .

Grapeseed Oil
Extracted from the seeds of grapes, typically wine grapes, grapeseed oil has a nutty flavor and can take high heat. It is typically used for stir-frying, deep-frying and in salad dressings and marinades.

Hazelnut Oil
Strongly flavored and darker than most vegetable oils, hazelnut oil is best used in salads, and in fish and poultry dishes. Though it has a high smoking point, it is high in saturated fat and calories, making it a poor choice for frying.

. . . . . . . . . . . . . . . . . . . . . . . . . . .

♥ Olive Oils
What is the difference between one kind of olive oil and another? Generally, the difference is the degree of acidity and the strength of flavor. Today, nearly all virgin and extra-virgin olive oils are cold-pressed from the first pressing of the olives, so that is not a significant factor. All olive oils should be stored away from heat and light, preferably in a dark glass container. Flavor peaks in the first year, so use it up!

- Virgin olive oil—sometimes labeled "pure olive oil" has a mild flavor and up to 2% acidity. It is best used when a subtle flavor is wanted, especially if you are going to infuse the oil with herbs.

- Extra virgin olive oil—the most expensive choice, it has less than 1% acidity and is the strongest tasting olive oil. It is good for all salad dressings and for sautéing when you need extra flavor in your dish.

- Light olive oil—is not lower in calories or fat! It is simply processed to have a light color and flavor. It also has a higher smoking point than other olive oils, so it's a good choice for sautéing or pan frying.

♥ Safflower Oil
Relatively tasteless and colorless, safflower oil can be used for salad dressing because it doesn't solidify when chilled. It has a relatively high smoking point, so you can use it for frying too.

. . . . . . . . . . . . . . . . . . . . . . . . . . .

Sesame Oil
Made from sesame seeds, the distinctive flavor of sesame oil contributes to the unique taste of Asian cooking.

. . . . . . . . . . . . . . . . . . . . . . . . . . .

Walnut Oil
The light, delicate flavor of walnut oil makes it perfect for salad dressings and other cold dishes. But don't use it for frying, as high heat makes it turn slightly bitter. Walnut oil is a good source of omega-3 fatty acids.

# {Create a Comfort Zone}

Never think that your kitchen is merely a place to prepare food. Listen to this fantastic, true

story, told to me by my friend Charlotte. Back many years ago, she had a friend who was

considering becoming a *baalas teshuvah*, an observant Jew. The young woman was urged

to go see Rebbetzin Sara Freifeld (a"h), wife of the Rosh Yeshiva in Far Rockaway at

the time. She was known as a scholar, teacher, and wise mentor in her own right. Born in

Jerusalem, she spoke with an accent, but you understood every word and were instantly

captured by her warmth.

Anyway, the potential BT had been given a big buildup about how this holy woman would

be able to guide her in her spiritual quest. So she made an appointment and went to Rebbetzin

Freifeld's house, as instructed. When she arrived, the *rebbetzin* called, "I'm here—the kitchen!

Just come right in." She found the *rebbetzin* sitting at the table with dozens of Formica

sample chips in front of her. She would hold up two or three of them together and look

around at the walls and counters. Before the girl could get out any of her profound questions,

Rebbetzin Freifeld asked, "What do you think? This or this? Which color would look

better here? What about that one?"

She was floored. This is the holy, spiritual woman everyone wanted her to see? She seemed like a regular housewife, stumped by mundane decorating decisions!

Sensing her disappointment, Rebbetzin Freifeld explained to her why these choices were so important—about how the atmosphere of her kitchen sets the tone for the entire household, how it influences the way visitors will perceive her home, her family, Judaism itself; how the food that comes out of this kitchen feeds innumerable guests and yeshiva students. By the end of her talk, the visitor was convinced that the destiny of Judaism was riding on the choice of Formica for that kitchen.

## make sure your kitchen is a place where everyone—cooks, kids, and company— all feel welcome.

So maybe you're thinking that your kitchen isn't the focal point for Jewish outreach in America, but think again. The sages tell us that every parent is charged with *"kiruv kerovim,"* drawing those close to us into the loving embrace of Judaism. You want your children to treasure *Yiddishkeit* as much as you do. So follow Rebbetzin Freifeld's example and make sure your kitchen is a place where everyone—cooks, kids, and company—all feel welcome.

Today's kitchens have turned from small areas relegated to the back of the house to the epicenter of the home. Family-friendly, eat-in dens are the new wave. Even if you can't reconstruct your home to accommodate this new style, you can make your kitchen—of any size—the magnet of your home.

Here are a few ideas to make it that cozy, go-to place in everyone's heart.

## Family Photos

Capture a memory, frame it, and hang it in your kitchen. It doesn't matter if you make a collage with your kids and get it laminated at Staples or indulge in the latest digital frame. (You can buy it with your anniversary gift money from mom-in-law. That's what I did!) You can put up several individual pictures in uniform gallery-style frames—thin black frames with mattes are nice. They needn't be expensive. Or go for an eclectic mismatch of eras, styles, shapes, and sizes and include pictures of your great-grandma (the one who walked across Europe to catch the boat to America) right alongside the newest member of your family.

One of my friends has a "Fun Family Wall" in her kitchen with an assortment of pictures of family trips, parties, and Purim antics spanning several decades. She says the idea is to remind her kids and grandkids of what a great life they have and how much fun it is to be part of their household. You can try this by framing individual pictures or using a corkboard.

But it's not only for the children. Cooking can be lonely or joyful, depending on how you look at it. Either way, pictures of your loved ones can bring a smile to your face, inspire your food, and remind you of why you're doing this in the first place.

## Artwork

My kitchen is called transitional— somewhere between modern and traditional—and I like things neat, sleek, and out of sight. But I have this one sliver of wall which is solely dedicated to my kids' projects and progress charts, and it's a wacky, colorful hodge-podge.

Progress charts are very popular just now. If you have young children, the charts are a real motivator. In my house, every time one of my children does a *mitzvah*, they get a sticker to paste on their chart. A full chart of stickers earns a prize. There are ready-made charts in the Jewish bookstores, or you can construct your own, emphasizing the *mitzvos* or character traits you want your particular young'uns to develop. ("Today I didn't pinch my little sister… I helped Mommy clean up the kitchen, even though it was yucky … I went to bed nicely and stayed in my pajamas…") One of my daughters is not entirely getting it and enjoys ripping her stickers off her chart to stick them elsewhere—so, in her case, a chart full of ripped-off stickers gets a prize.

I'm bummed that I didn't get a magnetic fridge because we all know that's the best place to display original kiddie crafts. Whether or not you have the space or aesthetic desire to hang things up, it's important to fuss over the crafts when they come in. Your child worked hard on that thing, so make a big deal about each masterpiece directly to him/ her and to visitors too, within earshot of the child. If you can't handle a cluttered looking fridge or kitchen wall, you can do what I do with overflow artwork: wall-paper the kids' rooms with their own projects.

## Advertise Healthy Snacks

To entice kids to open the refrigerator and find healthy snacks, get a little blackboard or a large pad of paper (better if magnetized, so it can be stuck on the fridge door), and advertise the good foods on hand. A friend of mine tried this on her teenagers to keep them from going directly to the high-carb snacks and steer them into the salads. Every week, she would scrawl on the black-board with chalk, as they do in the grocery stores. For example:

Check out today's specials!
* peaches
* cherries
* crunchy carrot sticks

Dunno if the kids went for it, but the adults in the household thought twice before digging into the bag of chips.

## Cookie Jars

On the flip side, life is not always about celery and soybeans. A cookie jar is a useful decorative item that can add charm and whimsy to any kitchen. Some people collect them, making a display of the many variations they've garnered on vacations or at craft stores. But even if you don't want your counters cluttered with this kind of memorabilia, one eye-catching cookie jar, brimming with everyone's favorites, always says "Welcome home!"

## Child-Size Grown-Up Stuff

If there's enough room in your kitchen, small, colorful tables and chairs make meal and snack times fun and they're great for coloring and games. My mom-in-law bought each of my children kiddie aprons with their names on them. What a gift! They love to wear them when they cook with me.

Yes, I do cook with my kids around. In fact, I make a point of it. I figure if I get them involved in cooking at an early age, they'll gain the kitchen confidence I never had. You can provide your children with their own kitchen utensils (plastic or silicone are best), so they can join you in meal prep. If they are too small to reach the counter, be sure to have a stepstool. In time, after you've been letting your children help in the kitchen for a while, you can create a kids' cookbook (with their input and artwork, of course) of their favorite recipes.

There are all kinds of ways children can participate in the kitchen. Peeling fruits or vegetables with a peeler is fairly safe and it makes them feel like they are really doing grown-up things. I give very young children jobs like taking scraps to the kitchen trashcan or bringing me things (even if they are within arm's reach).

And, of course, decorating comes naturally to children, so keep lots of sprinkles, chips, and other edible trimmings on hand so they can be creative. I let my kids decorate the challahs we bake with blue edible sparkles, colored sprinkles, or chocolate chips—even all at the same time—if that's what pleases them. Your husband will get used to cutting into a chocolate chip challah—believe me—and it's a small price to pay for fostering lifelong cooking joy.

## My friend told me a story

about her four-year-old grand-daughter proudly showing her a cake that she had brought over for *Shabbos*. "I made it!" the child reported happily. "Wow! It's beautiful," the grandma said. "Did you put the ingredients in the bowl yourself?"

"No. Mommy did that."
"Did you mix the batter?"
"No, Mommy did that too."
"Well, you surely didn't take it out of the oven, did you?"
  "Oh, no, it was much too hot for me to touch."
"So what did you do?"
"I had a very special job. I was the watcher!"

Well, that's a job too. Official "Taster" is another good one. So whether your children participate as the watchers, the tasters, the bringers or the mixers, they will feel comfortable in your kitchen at any age, because they know they are a part of everything going on in there.

Guests will feel at home too, if you create a physical atmosphere that is relaxed and inviting. If they offer to lend a hand, give 'em a cutting board. If they've simply wandered into your kitchen (because it looks and smells so good!), tell them to pull up a chair or bar stool, then offer a drink and some good conversation. With the right paint color, décor, and family-friendly ambiance, maybe you too can save the world (or at least, your little corner of it) right from your kitchen.

Tzedakah Boxes
Display them all over the house and in the kitchen; they transmit such an important lesson. Our family favorite is the "Thank You for Not Speaking *Loshon Hara*"—gossiping—box from the Chofetz Chaim Heritage Foundation used as a bookend for my cookbooks. (And yes, I've got tons of cookbooks and they're not just multiple copies of mine!) Charity boxes are the hallmark of a Jewish home, so show that you're proud of them. Having them visible is also a good reminder to give your children a few coins to put in the boxes every day.

Greenery
Flowers and plants are a really great way to warm up a space. I play around with different colors and vases—short and modern and square, with rocks at the bottom—or using a ceramic pitcher that looks like it was picked up at a crafts fair or a flea market. A rustic container like that makes it look like the flowers in them were just cut from your garden. (You should know me well enough by now to know that I only have a green thumb when I stick my hands in the kids' finger paint.)

If you're buying plants for your home, check with the florist to make sure they're not toxic, if eaten. If he tells you, "Nobody eats houseplants!" just point to your two-year-old, smile sweetly and insist, "You never met my little leaf-eater." If your florist doesn't know which plants are dangerous, check with your local poison control center.

# {Before We Start}

I've tried to be as accurate as I can with the times—nudging, cajoling, and haranguing both professional and home cooks to triple test each recipe. We recorded their times like athletes training for the Olympics, practically in milliseconds. The final times recorded are the average times it took all the recipe testers. They are pretty accurate estimates but keep in mind that no two people take exactly the same time to mince an onion or chop a pepper.

In some recipes, I mention specific brands for some ingredients: they're the brands I trust and love to use. And because quality products are my passion, I made it a point to interview some of the fascinating people who create them, sharing their stories and food advice in a special section of this book called "Spotlight—What's New in Kosher." I think "cooking secrets" are so passé. I want you to be in the know!

The prep times in this book assume a few things:

- **Your pot of boiling water, if called for, is already boiling.** Tip: Put up a large pot of water to boil when you get home from work or 15 minutes before you plan to start your meal prep.

- **Your oven is preheated to the desired temperature.** Heat your oven when you walk into the kitchen, so it has time to reach the correct temperature while you're preparing the food.

- **Frozen ingredients that needed to be thawed beforehand are ready.** A great tip: Thaw frozen vegetables in a cold water bath and drain just before using so they won't be soggy.

- **All of your ingredients are in front of you before you begin to cook.** Official "prep time" cannot include time spent searching for ancho chili powder, only to realize that you have none and now you have to call your neighbor or run to the store. Many of my recipes call for fun new ingredients that may not be staples (yet!) in your pantry or fridge. Plan your menus and shopping lists beforehand to make sure you have everything you'll need. Of course, you can get it all at Kosher.com.

- **Multi-tasking is the key to meals in minutes.** A (multi-tasking) tip will precede recipes when applicable. The recipes for each meal are designed to work together to ensure that your entire meal is ready on time.

# { If You've Got 20 Minutes }

We all have those days when time collapses and you simply don't have a minute to think of meals, much less have them cooked and ready when the family gets home.

It happens to me all the time. And I'll admit it's because my biggest problem in life is my lack of organization. Although I work in the food industry—from writing cookbooks to marketing for Kosher.com—I still don't think about supper until my stomach is grumbling.

So if you happen to remember at the last minute that
your entire extended family, plus your kid's school marching band,
is coming to din-din, you'll still be set!

By nature, I am a last-minute person, day to day and minute to minute, even when it comes to commitments I've made. I'm lucky if, at around noon, I remember that I promised to cook dinner for my neighbor who just had a baby. I'll be sorting some laundry, or picking up a carpool, and suddenly, "Omigosh!" it hits me—and I get that sinking sensation in my gut. "What's today? Is this Wednesday? Wednesday! Isn't this the day I said I'd bring over supper for her kids, all eight of them?"

It's not that I don't try to be organized. I have four wall calendars, two electronic calendars, plus three notebooks in which I religiously record my upcoming tasks. Then there are 10 random scraps of paper and several yellow Post-it notes on my bathroom mirror reminding me to check my To-Do lists. The problem is that the doctor appointments are on one calendar, a business meeting is on another, and hubby's birthday is on yet another.

A girl who has obviously inherited faulty "organization genes" needs a book that plans meals. So it's no exaggeration to say that I wrote this book for myself and I figure that I'm not the *only* one in the world longing for a problem solver! So if you happen to remember at the last minute that your entire extended family, plus your kid's school marching band, is coming to din-din, you'll still be set.

But you've got to keep calm. I once met a woman who was the mother of 11 kids and she was definitely physiologically predisposed to calmness. But even with all that calm in her genes, I figured there still had to be a few pearls of wisdom she could share that even I, ever-stressed Jamie, could *attempt* to work into my life.

So I asked her—in my common way of asking everyone I meet (whether I know the person well or just sat next to her at the nail salon)—what are the answers to life's secrets, what are the keys to happiness? And I share—as I am known to do—all my very personal stresses and worries, shortcomings and fears, as I do with my closest friends, mother-in-law, and readers of this book.

Do you want to know her secret for happiness? How this mother of 11 kids keeps a perpetual smile on her face? "Cereal for dinner."

Literally—that's what she said to me. She never worries about dinner, just pulls out the milk and corn flakes. I wouldn't have believed her, except that my sister-in-law, once (and I emphasize, once) slaved over a fancy steak dinner. While waiting for this culinary miracle, her husband browsed the cupboards and saw FRUITY PEBBLES! *"Fruity Pebbles!"* he screamed, "We never buy Fruity Pebbles! Um, honey—can you save the steak for tomorrow?"

Ok, so I tried it. One particularly busy day, when hubby wanted to know what's for dinner, I said "Cereal." He choked down a gasp, but in his great wisdom, guess what he suggested: breakfast for dinner!

"Let's have Omelet Night," he said cheerfully. Now, while not as easy as cereal, you have to admit that quick-prep foods usually relegated to breakfast could work. Who ever decreed that eggs could be eaten only before noon?

Take, for example, the Fines Herbes Omelet, pronounced by those in the know as "feen 'erb" not "fines herbs." (I can tell you this because I was once not in the know, and now that I *am* in the know, I can bring you such information. Notice that I'm using the French spelling for the herbs, which gives me credibility in high places. But as a dyed-in-the-wool American patriot, I can't bring myself to write "omelette" instead of our good ol' American "omelet." There are some lines even I won't cross.)

"Fines herbes" is a mixture of finely chopped herbs, usually parsley, chervil, tarragon, and chives. So the Fines Herbes Omelet, if made correctly, can be an exquisite culinary experience. I know a chef—someone so famous you would recognize his name in an instant—who uses this dish as a test for cooks who work in his restaurant kitchens worldwide. His theory is that if you can make a delicate and creamy, perfectly balanced Fines Herbes Omelet, you can make anything.

## If you can make a delicate and creamy, perfectly balanced Fines Herbes Omelet, you can make anything.

While I never worked in his kitchen, I have learned the tricks of his trade, the little touches that could bring my omelets to the table at any posh dining locale. And guess what? It takes just a few minutes (unless you're serving 11 children you've personally brought into this world—in which case, you will need more than a Fines Herbes Omelet to help you make it through the day!) It's a total low-carb, low-sugar, dream dish, high in protein and iron. A bit of goat cheese and a simple, light salad round out this meal. Voila! You've transformed a "breakfast" food into a superb dinner that will rate high on everyone's list of favorites in less than 20 minutes!

So whether you're planning-challenged, as I am, or you've got everything in perfect order but you're just having a crazy, impossibly busy day—the super-quick recipes in the following chapter are just what you need *right now!*

{20} minute meals

# { Asian Chicken Salad }
## Iced Ginger Green Tea

**Serves 4** | Start steeping the tea when the noodles are baking.

## Asian Chicken Salad

*To make this delicious salad, buy a BBQ Roasted Chicken from Kosher.com or use leftover roast chicken.*

- 1 **(3-ounce) package ramen soup noodles**
- 2 **tablespoons chili sauce**
- ¼ **to ½ cup bottled carrot ginger dressing**
- 1 **cube frozen crushed ginger, thawed, or 1 teaspoon ground ginger**
- 1 **cube frozen chopped cilantro, thawed, or 1 teaspoon finely chopped cilantro**
- 1 **cup snow peas, trimmed, rinsed, and dried**
- 1 **(5-ounce) package mesclun mix salad, rinsed and dried**
- 3 **cups shredded rotisserie chicken, about a 3-pound chicken**
- 1 **medium red onion, halved lengthwise and thinly sliced**
- 1 **(11-ounce) can mandarin orange segments, drained**
- 2 **tablespoons sesame seeds**
- 2 **scallions, sliced diagonally**

Preheat oven to 350° F.

Fill a large pot three-quarters full with water and bring to a rolling boil. While the water is heating, break up ramen noodles and place them on a jelly-roll pan. Bake for about 8 minutes until toasted.

While noodles are baking, make dressing: In a small bowl, whisk together chili sauce, salad dressing, ginger, and cilantro. Set aside.

Fill a large bowl about three-quarters full with cold water and ice cubes. To blanch the snow peas: Place them into the boiling water for 30 seconds; drain them and immediately plunge them into the ice water to stop cooking. When snow peas are completely cool, drain and dry them.

To compose salad: Place greens in a large bowl. Add snow peas, chicken, onion, mandarin oranges, sesame seeds, and toasted ramen noodles.

Pour dressing over salad and toss. Garnish with scallions and serve with Iced Ginger Green Tea.

## Iced Ginger Green Tea

*Ginger has been used in cooking for almost 3,000 years by Babylonians, Egyptians, Persians, Chinese, and Japanese. Crystallized ginger is fresh ginger that has been cooked in a sugar syrup. It is available in the dried fruit section of the supermarket, in Asian markets, and in health food stores. Ginger is a great remedy for upset stomachs!*

- 1 **quart water**
- 3 **green tea bags**
- 1 **tablespoon finely chopped crystallized ginger**

In a medium saucepan over medium heat, bring water to a boil. Place tea bags and crystallized ginger in the water. Steep for 10 minutes. Strain and serve over ice in tall glasses.

**Recommended Wine:**
**Baron Herzog Pinot Grigio**

The medley of flavors and spice in this Asian-inspired meal calls for a crisp refreshing white wine, possibly even one with a hint of sweetness.

# { Beef and Green Bean Stir-Fry }

Serves 6

## Beef and Green Bean Stir-Fry

*Stir-fry is an Asian cooking method using very high heat and a very small amount of oil. It is essential that you have all of the ingredients ready—sliced, chopped, and measured—before you begin to work.*

- 1 ¼ **pounds skirt steak, thinly sliced across the grain**
- ¼ **cup Mikee Chinese Marinade with Garlic**
- 3 **cups water**
- 3 **cups instant rice (white or brown)**
- 2 **tablespoons canola oil**
- 1 **cup fresh green beans, rinsed, and trimmed**
- 2 **cloves garlic, minced**
- 2 **scallions, sliced**

In a large bowl, place steak in the marinade. Marinate, uncovered, for 10 minutes, at room temperature.

While meat is marinating, prepare rice: In a large saucepan, bring water to boil. Stir in rice and cover. Remove from heat and set aside.

Remove meat from marinade and discard marinade. In a wok or large sauté pan over high heat, heat oil until smoking. Cook meat, stirring, for 30 seconds. Add green beans, stirring, for 5 minutes more.

Add remaining minced garlic. Keep heat high while continuing to stir. Continue cooking for another 2 minutes.

Spoon rice into a large serving bowl. Serve Stir-Fry over rice; garnish with scallions.

## I Love Chinese Food

*When my mother was pregnant with me, she religiously frequented a Chinese restaurant for dinner. For the first 5 years of my life, I couldn't get enough Chinese food. To this day, I still love it. Here's my "Quick & Kosher" beef stir-fry. An accomplishment above and beyond getting this dish right is learning how to eat it—along with every single grain of rice—with chopsticks. For a lesson on that, I'm afraid you'll need another book.*

**Recommended Wine:**
**Binyamina Zinfandel**

Though beef is often associated with cabernet, the sweet marinade will pair well with a robust red with sweet tannins.

# { Bowties with Salmon and Peas in Lemon Dill Sauce }
## Melon Salad

**Serves 6** | Prepare the Melon Salad while the pasta is cooking.

## Bowties with Salmon and Peas in Lemon Dill Sauce

*The combination of pasta and salmon seasoned with onions and lemon makes a tasty dish that would be a nice main course for a luncheon or a family dinner.*

1   (1-pound) box bowtie pasta
2   (7 ½-ounce) cans salmon
1   medium red onion, coarsely chopped
1   cup Gefen Regular or Lite Mayonnaise
½   teaspoon lemon zest
3   tablespoons freshly squeezed lemon juice
2   tablespoons chopped fresh dill
½   teaspoon garlic powder
½   teaspoon freshly ground black pepper
1   cup frozen peas, thawed

Cook pasta according to package instructions. Drain well.

While pasta is cooking, drain salmon. Place salmon into a mixing bowl, remove bones and break into chunks. Add onions and pasta to salmon. Combine well by gently tossing.

In a small bowl, prepare the creamy lemon sauce by whisking together the mayonnaise, lemon zest, lemon juice, dill, garlic powder, and pepper.

Pour the sauce over the salmon and pasta and toss gently. Add peas. Toss gently once more and serve with Melon Salad.

## Melon Salad

*Buying fruit that is already cut up saves time.*

2   cups store-bought cubed watermelon
2   cups store-bought cubed cantaloupe
2   cups store-bought cubed honeydew melon
2   tablespoons freshly squeezed lime juice
½   cup chopped fresh mint

In a large bowl, combine melons, lime juice, and mint. Cover and chill until serving.

## Thawing Veggies

*A great way to thaw vegetables is to place them in a bowl of cold water for about 3 minutes and drain.*

**Recommended Wine:**
**Baron Herzog Chardonnay**

Though salmon can be paired with many wines, here the lemon dill sauce dominates and calls for a crisp and refreshing white with similar flavors.

# { Chicken Tacos }
## Hot Pepper Iced Tea

**Serves 4** | Yield 12 Tacos

## Chicken Tacos

*This is an easy Mexican-style dinner for a perfect kid-friendly fiesta.*

- 3 **cups shredded rotisserie chicken, about a 3-pound chicken**
- 1 **(15-ounce) jar mild salsa, divided**
- 2 **tomatoes, diced**
- 1 **tablespoon freshly squeezed lime juice**
- 2 **tablespoons chopped fresh cilantro**
- 12 **yellow corn taco shells**
- 1 **cup canned black beans, rinsed and drained**
- 1 **avocado, pitted, peeled, and diced**
- 2 **cups shredded iceberg lettuce (½ head), rinsed and dried**
- **Soy sour cream**

In a large sauté pan over medium heat, cook shredded chicken with 1 cup salsa.

In a medium bowl, toss tomatoes with lime juice and cilantro.

To assemble tacos, lay out all 12 tacos on a work surface. Evenly distribute the chicken, then beans, then avocado, then lettuce, and finally the tomato mixture among the tacos.

Serve tacos with sides of sour cream, the remaining salsa, and Hot Pepper Iced Tea.

## Hot Pepper Iced Tea

- 1 **quart prepared iced tea**
- ¼ **teaspoon cayenne pepper**

Pour iced tea into a large pitcher; stir in cayenne pepper. Let sit for 5 minutes. Stir and pour into ice-filled glasses.

Recommended Wine:
**Carmel Appellation Cabernet Franc**

Rotisserie chicken has robust flavors that hold up nicely to red wines; while the salsa, cilantro and tomatoes in this dish call for a wine with lively acidity.

# { Fettuccine Alfredo with Peas }

## Simple Salad with Basic Vinaigrette

. . . . . . . . . . . . . . . . . . . . . . . . . . . . . . . . . . . . . . . . . . . . . . . . . . . . . . . . . . . . . . . . . . . . . . . . . . . .

**Serves 4** | Thaw peas for about 3 minutes in a bath of cold water and drain. This way they won't become soggy.

## Fettuccine Alfredo with Peas

*This is a dish best made to taste. The trick to success in alfredo dishes is coating your noodles to your liking. I like a creamy and cheesy alfredo—and even double this sauce recipe when I'm feeling sinful. You can adjust the amount of cheese and cream to achieve the consistency you prefer.*

- 1 (1-pound) box fettuccine
- 1 cup heavy cream
- 1/4 pound butter, at room temperature, cut into 8 pieces
- 1 cup Natural & Kosher Grated Parmesan
- 1 teaspoon freshly ground black pepper
- 1 cup frozen green peas, thawed (optional)

Cook fettuccine according to package instructions.

While pasta is cooking, heat the cream in a medium saucepan over medium heat. Do not let the cream come to a boil. Whisk in butter until melted. Add the Parmesan, whisking continually, until sauce thickens. Keep warm over low heat, stirring occasionally. Be careful not to burn the sauce.

Drain pasta; do not rinse. Place in a bowl large enough to allow tossing. Pour sauce over warm pasta and toss to coat.

Sprinkle with pepper and toss in the peas. Top with additional Parmesan, if desired. Serve immediately with Simple Salad with Basic Vinaigrette.

## Simple Salad with Basic Vinaigrette

- 1/3 cup red wine vinegar
- 1 tablespoon freshly squeezed lemon juice
- 1 tablespoon honey
- 1 tablespoon minced shallot or onion
- 2/3 cup extra virgin olive oil
- 1/2 teaspoon kosher salt
- 1/4 teaspoon freshly ground black pepper
- 1 (5-ounce) package mixed salad greens, rinsed and dried

Place vinegar, lemon juice, honey, and shallots in blender or food processor. With the blender or processor running, slowly add olive oil. Add salt and pepper.

Slowly add as much of the vinaigrette as you like to the salad greens while lightly tossing, being especially careful not to bruise the greens.

. . . . . . . . . . . . . . . . . . . . . . . . . . . . . . . .

**Recommended Wine:**
**Castel "C" Blanc**

This rich creamy dish is a no-brainer complement to a creamy chardonnay.

# { Fines Herbes Goat Cheese Omelet }
## Mixed Green Salad

## Fines Herbes Goat Cheese Omelet

*This is such a quick fabulous meal with just a simple mixed green salad on the side.*

- 3 large eggs
  Pinch kosher salt
  Pinch freshly ground black pepper
- 1 tablespoon butter
- 1 tablespoon fines herbes (see recipe below)
- 1 tablespoon Natural & Kosher Natural Chèvre, crumbled
  Fresh herbs to garnish (optional)

In a medium bowl, beat eggs well with salt and pepper to taste.

Heat butter in an omelet pan or small sauté pan over medium heat. Do not let butter brown. When butter starts to foam, pour eggs into the pan. Stir them with the back of a fork, stirring over the whole surface of the pan. A thin layer of eggs should begin to set. At this point, sprinkle fines herbes and goat cheese over the eggs. Let the eggs finish cooking without touching them, about 2-3 minutes. The eggs are done when they are set and no longer runny.

Remove pan from heat. Gently slide a spatula under the edge of the eggs and fold them in half. Slide the omelet onto a serving plate.

Garnish with fresh herbs if desired. Serve with Mixed Green Salad.

## Mixed Green Salad

- 1 cup mixed baby greens, rinsed and dried
- 1 tablespoon freshly squeezed lemon juice
- ½ teaspoon kosher salt
- ¼ teaspoon cracked black pepper
- 2 tablespoons extra virgin olive oil

Place greens in a serving bowl. Whisk together lemon juice, salt, and pepper. While whisking, pour in oil in a slow stream. Pour dressing over greens. Toss and serve.

## What is "Fines Herbes"?

*Fines herbes is a mixture of equal parts of the following fresh or dried herbs: chervil, chives, parsley, and tarragon. Chervil is a delicate herb that has been hard to find, however it is starting to show up more and more in farmers markets and in local supermarkets. If you can't find chervil, just add more of the other herbs.*

45

**Recommended Wine:**
**Elvi Adar Brut Cava**

The combination of eggs, cheese, herbs, and pepper is complex and can be challenging to pair with wines. Sparkling wine, however, goes with all foods and works great here.

# { Grilled Vegetable Wraps }
## Creamy Coleslaw

**Serves 4**

## Grilled Vegetable Wraps

*To save time, purchase your vegetables already grilled
from Kosher.com or your local supermarket.*

- 1 **pound store-bought grilled vegetables**
- 1 **cup herbed cream cheese spread,
  at room temperature**
- 4 **(8-inch) whole wheat flour tortillas**

Place tortillas on a work surface. Spread ¼ cup cream
cheese evenly over each tortilla, leaving about a 1-inch
border. Distribute the vegetables evenly among the
tortillas.

To roll up wraps: Fold in the right and left sides,
enclosing the veggies. Starting from the bottom,
gently roll up the tortilla, ending with the
seam-side down. Cut each wrap in half.

Serve plated with Creamy Coleslaw.

## Creamy Coleslaw

- 1 **(16-ounce) package coleslaw mix**
- 1 **small onion, finely diced**
- 1 **cup Gefen Regular or Lite Mayonnaise**
- ¼ **cup regular or low-fat sour cream**
- 1 **teaspoon kosher salt**
- ½ **teaspoon freshly ground black pepper**

Mix all ingredients together in a large bowl.

**Recommended Wine:**
**Baron Herzog Chenin Blanc**

The smokiness of the grilled veggies and
the creaminess of the cream cheese spread
and coleslaw will go wonderfully with a
chenin blanc.

# { Individual Whole Wheat Tortilla Pizzas }
## Crudités with Creamy Italian Dressing

**Serves 4** | Arrange the crudités platter while pizzas are baking.

## Individual Whole Wheat Tortilla Pizzas

*Pizzas can be made with any type of bread: pitas, English muffins, bagels, even matzoh. Here I use whole wheat tortillas as the base.*

   **Gefen Canola Oil Cooking Spray**
1  **(10-ounce) package frozen chopped spinach, thawed**
1  **cup Natural & Kosher Ricotta**
4  **(8-inch) whole wheat tortillas**
1  **small red pepper, ribs and seeds removed, cut into strips**
1  **small red onion, thinly sliced**
1  **cup Natural & Kosher Shredded Mozzarella**
12  **fresh basil leaves, torn**

Preheat oven to 375° F. Lightly spray a baking sheet.

Squeeze the liquid from spinach and place spinach in a large bowl. Mix in the ricotta cheese.

Place tortillas on the prepared baking sheet. Evenly layer spinach mixture, peppers, onions, mozzarella, and basil among the tortillas.

Bake for 9 to 12 minutes.

Arrange on a serving platter and serve with Crudités with Creamy Italian Dressing.

## Crudités with Creamy Italian Dressing

*It is easy to assemble a crudité platter. Many produce sections now offer already prepared vegetables; if you use them, this dish takes almost no time at all!.*

4  **cups assorted cut vegetables such as carrot sticks, cherry tomatoes, celery sticks, and cucumber slices**
1  **cup bottled creamy Italian dressing**

Arrange cut vegetables on a platter around a small bowl of dressing and serve.

. . . . . . . . . . . . . . . . . . . . . . . . . . . . . . . . .
**Recommended Wine:**
**Ovadia Estates Chianti**

Pizza—the quintessential Italian meal that pairs wonderfully with a good Italian Chianti.

# { Mexican Burgers with Flour Tortillas }

## Rice with Corn and Peppers

**Serves 4** | While burgers are cooking, prepare Rice with Corn and Peppers.

## Mexican Burgers with Flour Tortillas

*If you really crave a bun with your burger, then go traditional. To warm tortillas: Microwave, covered with a damp paper towel, for 20 to 30 seconds on medium.*

- 1 **pound ground beef**
- 1 **poblano pepper, seeded and finely diced**
- 2 **tablespoons ketchup**
- ½ **teaspoon ancho chili powder**
- ½ **cup canned black beans, rinsed and drained**
- 1 **teaspoon kosher salt**
- ¾ **cup store-bought guacamole**
- 1 **(4-ounce) can green chilies, chopped (optional)**
- 8 **(6-inch) flour tortillas, torn into large pieces**

Heat grill or sauté pan.

In a large bowl, mix ground beef with poblano, ketchup, chili powder, black beans, and salt. Shape into 4 patties.

On the grill or in a large sauté pan, cook burgers over medium heat on each side for 5 minutes for medium doneness, 6 to 7 minutes for well done. Transfer to a serving platter.

Place 2 tablespoons guacamole on top of each burger. If desired, place green chili peppers on top.

Serve with warm flour tortillas to sop up the sauce and Rice with Corn and Peppers.

## Rice with Corn and Peppers

- **Gefen Canola Oil Cooking Spray**
- ½ **cup finely chopped red pepper, ribs and seeds removed (about ½ medium pepper)**
- 1 **(11-ounce) can shoepeg or other white corn**
- **Kosher salt**
- **Freshly ground black pepper**
- 2 **cups Manischewitz All Natural Chicken Broth**
- 2 **cups instant rice**

Spray a small sauté pan with cooking spray.

Over medium heat, cook peppers until soft, about 5 minutes. Add corn and heat through. Season with salt and pepper to taste.

In a separate medium saucepan, bring broth to a boil. Add rice, stir, cover, and remove from heat. Let sit for 5 minutes.

Stir corn and peppers into rice and serve.

**Recommended Wine:**
**Herzog Selection Brut Rosé**

These Mexican burgers with their hot peppers, chili powder, and green chilies can be HOT. The best way to cool down your palate is with a cool sparkling rosé.

# { Mozzarella Mushroom Burgers }
## Quick Gazpacho

**Serves 6** | Gazpacho is best served chilled. To save time chilling, keep the boxed broth and cucumber in the fridge. Make the gazpacho while the mushrooms are grilling. Chill until serving.

## Mozzarella Mushroom Burgers

*This dish is a perfect vegetarian burger option. The creaminess of the cheese perfectly complements the earthiness of the mushrooms.*

Gefen Canola Oil Cooking Spray

6 portabella mushroom caps, each 3- to 4-inches in diameter

¼ cup Bartenura Balsamic Vinegar

¼ cup olive oil

Kosher salt

Freshly ground black pepper

6 slices Natural & Kosher Mozzarella

12 slices crusty bread

1 (16-ounce) jar roasted red peppers, drained, dried with paper towels, and cut into strips

Spray grill pan with cooking spray and place over high heat.

To prepare mushrooms for grilling: Remove the stems. Use a spoon to remove the gills by running it along the bottoms of the mushrooms. Wipe clean with paper towels.

In a small bowl, whisk together balsamic vinegar, olive oil, and salt and pepper to taste. Brush the mixture on both sides of each mushroom with a pastry brush.

When grill pan is very hot, place mushrooms in the pan, gill side up. Baste mushrooms with the vinegar and oil mixture. Cook for 8 minutes. Turn and cook second side for 6 minutes. Place a mozzarella slice on top of each mushroom cap and continue cooking for another 1 to 2 minutes to melt cheese.

To assemble: Place mushrooms, cheese side up, on a slice of bread. Evenly distribute roasted red pepper slices on the cheese and place a second slice of bread on top.

Serve with Quick Gazpacho.

## Quick Gazpacho

1 large English cucumber, peeled, seeded, and cut in chunks

½ medium red onion, coarsely chopped

½ cup torn cilantro leaves

1 (32-ounce) box of tomato soup

In a blender or food processor, place cucumbers, onions, and cilantro.

While the blender is running, pour in the tomato soup. Purée until smooth. Chill until serving.

53

**Recommended Wine:**
**Carmel single vineyard "Kayoumi" Shiraz**

The earthy and almost gamey nature of portabella mushrooms works great with an earthy Syrah (AKA "Shiraz").

# { Pan-Seared Tuna with Lemon, Capers, and Olives }

## Orzo with Feta and Basil

**Serves 2** | While tuna is cooking, prepare orzo.

## Pan-Seared Tuna with Lemon, Capers, and Olives

 2  cloves garlic

¼  cup capers, drained

½  cup assorted pitted olives, drained

 1  teaspoon kosher salt

½  teaspoon cracked black pepper

 2  lemons, halved and seeded

 2  (8-ounce) tuna steaks

 2  tablespoons olive oil

In the bowl of a food processor or blender, place garlic, capers, olives, salt, and pepper. Blend until it becomes a paste.

Squeeze lemons over tuna. Smear garlic paste on both sides of each tuna steak. Heat olive oil in a sauté pan over medium heat. When oil is shimmering, place tuna in the pan; reduce heat to low. Cook for 3 minutes on each side for medium doneness. Keep an eye on the garlic paste to make sure it doesn't burn.

Serve with Orzo with Feta and Basil.

## Orzo with Feta and Basil

½  pound orzo

 2  cups Manischewitz All Natural Vegetable Broth

½  pound Greek-style feta, crumbled

¼  cup chopped basil

Cook orzo according to package instructions, using vegetable broth instead of water.

Transfer orzo to a large bowl and toss with feta and basil.

**Recommended Wine:**
**Barkan Classic Pinot Noir**

Tuna is hearty enough to stand up to a red wine, but the brininess of the capers and olives really require something light and juicy.

# { Stir-Fried Tofu with Soba Noodles }

## Baby Bok Choy

Serves 4

## Stir-Fried Tofu with Soba Noodles

*Soba noodles, which are made from buckwheat, originated in Japan where it isn't considered bad manners to slurp the noodles.*

- 1 (8 ½ - ounce) package soba noodles
- 2 tablespoons canola oil
- 1 (14-ounce) container firm tofu, cut in ¾ - inch cubes, drained on paper towels
- 2 cloves garlic, minced or 2 cubes frozen Gefen Crushed Garlic
- ½ cup ginger teriyaki sauce
- ½ cup water
- 1 cup frozen shelled edamame, thawed
- 2 scallions, thinly sliced diagonally

Cook noodles according to package instructions.

In a wok or large sauté pan, heat canola oil over high heat. Add tofu and brown on all sides, about 5 minutes. Add garlic and gently mix to combine. Cook for 1 minute and add noodles. Toss noodles with tofu and garlic.

Add ginger teriyaki sauce and toss. Add water by the tablespoon, if needed, to fully coat the noodles and tofu with sauce. Add edamame and scallions. Toss gently and heat through.

Serve immediately with Baby Bok Choy.

## Baby Bok Choy

*Baby bok choy is a younger, more tender version of bok choy and has a sweeter, lighter taste. Baby bok choy can be used whole or cut up, but regular bok choy must be cut up.*

- 1 tablespoon canola oil
- 4 heads baby bok choy, rinsed, dried, and sliced lengthwise
- 1 cube frozen crushed ginger
- ½ tablespoon soy sauce

Heat oil in a large sauté pan over high heat. Add bok choy and ginger. Cook, stirring, for 2 to 3 minutes, or until bok choy is just tender. Add soy sauce and mix well. Spoon onto serving plate and serve.

**Recommended Wine:**
**Jeunesse Chardonnay**

This light and healthful dish of delicate noodles and tofu calls for a delicate wine, while the ginger teriyaki sauce can be complemented by something a little sweet.

# { Three Cheese Pita Panini }
## Simple Greens with Basil Vinaigrette

Serves 4 | Prepare salad while panini are grilling.

## Three Cheese Pita Panini

*This is easy, easy, easy. Panini should be grilled over medium heat. If the temperature is too high the bread will toast and the cheese won't melt. If you don't have grill pans, just use sauté pans for grilling the panini.*

- 8 **(7-inch) pitas without pockets**
- 4 **tablespoons hummus**
- 4 **tablespoons Moroccan matbucha**
- 4 **slices Les Petites Fermieres Havarti**
- 4 **slices Les Petites Fermieres Swiss**
- 8 **slices red onion**
- 8 **slices on-the-vine tomatoes**
- 8 **whole basil leaves**
- 4 **slices Natural & Kosher Fresh Mozzarella**
  **Gefen Canola Oil Cooking Spray**

Preheat oven to 250° F.

Lay out 4 pitas on a work surface. Spread 1 tablespoon hummus and 1 tablespoon matbucha on each pita. Top with 1 slice Havarti, 1 slice Swiss, 2 slices onion, 2 slices tomato, and 2 basil leaves. Place 1 slice mozzarella on top. Cover with a second pita.

Spray 2 grill pans with cooking spray and place over medium heat. When pans are hot, place panini in the pans and weigh each down with a heavy pot lid or cast iron pan. Grill for 3 minutes on each side. Transfer to a baking sheet and place in the oven to keep warm. Repeat with remaining 2 panini.

Serve with Simple Greens with Basil Vinaigrette.

## Simple Greens with Basil Vinaigrette

*A 5-ounce package of lettuces gives you about 8 cups— and ¾ cup dressing is just the right amount.*

- ½ **cup bottled Italian vinaigrette**
- ¼ **cup chopped basil leaves**
- 1 **(5-ounce) package of baby green lettuces, rinsed and dried**

In a blender, combine vinaigrette and basil. Purée for a few minutes until the dressing is well blended. Place greens in a large bowl and toss with dressing.

**Recommended Wine:**
**Binyamina Shiraz Reserve**

A nice herbaceous Syrah will go great with the fresh basil and cheese in these dishes.

# { Vegetable Cheese Quesadillas with Rice and Beans }

**Serves 4** | Using a pizza wheel makes it easy to cut the quesadillas.

## Vegetable Cheese Quesadillas with Rice and Beans

*For homemade guacamole recipe, see page 205.*

1   **cup Texmati Rice and Beans**
8   **(10-inch) tortillas, any variety**
2   **cups Les Petites Fermieres Shredded Cheddar**
2   **cups store-bought julienned vegetables**
    **Gefen Canola Oil Cooking Spray**
1   **(12-ounce) jar mild salsa**
1   **(8-ounce) container guacamole**
1   **(16-ounce) container regular or low-fat sour cream**

Preheat oven to 250° F.

Prepare rice and beans according to the package instructions.

Lay out tortillas on a work surface. Sprinkle ¼ cup cheese over half of each tortilla. Top with ¼ cup vegetables. Fold the other half of the tortilla over the filling.

Spray a large sauté pan with cooking spray. Heat the pan over medium heat until hot. Place two tortillas side by side in the pan. Cook for 1 to 2 minutes on each side until cheese is melted. Transfer the tortillas to a cutting board and cut each into three wedges. Keep warm in the oven while you cook remaining tortillas, two at a time.

Top tortillas with salsa, guacamole, and sour cream. Serve with the rice and beans.

## What's a Quesadilla?

*The number one question I'm always asked is "How do you pronounce that?" Answer: kay-sa-DEE-ya. This Spanish word literally means "cheese in a tortilla." It's a Mexican food made primarily of cheese folded inside a tortilla and cooked until the cheese melts, like a Mexican version of grilled cheese. But there are no rules; you can add more ingredients or forget the cheese altogether and fold the tortilla over any fillings of your choice. Pizza Quesadillas are a hit with the kids—all you need is marinara sauce and Mozzarella. I have a great recipe in this book for upscale Blueberry Cheese Quesadillas (made with fresh blueberries, peaches, and goat cheese, page 81). My all-time favorite is from my first book, Quick & Kosher: Recipes From The Bride Who Knew Nothing; Chocolate Quesadillas, page 237, just oozing with peanut butter, melted chocolate, and marshmallow—divine! Wonder if that's what the Mexicans had in mind?*

**Recommended Wine:**
**Herzog Reserve Late Harvest Chenin Blanc**

Strong and diverse flavors such as those found in cheddar cheese, salsa, sour cream and guacamole clash with most wines, red and white. A well-balanced sweet wine, however, is a magical elixir for this medley.

# { Whole Wheat Spaghetti and Goat Cheese Crumble }

## Baby Lettuces with Raspberry Vinaigrette

........................................................................................

**Serves 6**

## Whole Wheat Spaghetti and Goat Cheese Crumble

*To save time, use a mandoline to cut your vegetables. The vegetable slices will then be of equal thickness and cook uniformly.*

- 1 **cup olive oil**
- 2 **cloves garlic, crushed**
- ¼ **cup fresh thyme leaves**
- 1 **(1-pound) box whole wheat thin spaghetti**
- 1 **sweet potato, peeled and cut into matchsticks**
- ½ **small red onion, thinly sliced**
- 2 **small zucchinis, sliced paper thin**
- 5 ½ **ounces Natural & Kosher Natural Chèvre**
- ½ **cup chopped walnuts**

Heat oil in a small saucepan, over low heat, with garlic and thyme leaves. Do not allow to boil.

In a large pot filled with 8 quarts of salted boiling water, cook spaghetti with sweet potato for 8 minutes or until desired tenderness.

While pasta and sweet potato are cooking, place onions and zucchini in a large serving bowl and crumble goat cheese into the bowl. Mix well.

When pasta and sweet potatoes are done, drain. Immediately pour hot pasta and sweet potatoes over goat cheese, onions, and zucchini. Toss to combine.

Drizzle infused oil over pasta and toss again.

Sprinkle chopped walnuts on top and serve with Baby Lettuces with Raspberry Vinaigrette.

## Baby Lettuces with Raspberry Vinaigrette

- 1 **(5-ounce) package baby lettuces, rinsed and dried**
- ½ **cup bottled raspberry vinaigrette**

Toss the greens with the vinaigrette in a large salad bowl.

## Infused Oils

*Cooking the herbs and garlic in the olive oil creates a savory and aromatic infused oil that can be used over pasta or in salad dressing. Infused oils can be safely stored in your refrigerator for one to two weeks.*

........................................................................................

**Recommended Wine:**

**Barkan Reserve Chardonnay**

With its sweet potato, whole wheat pasta, and goat cheese, this dish will pair very nicely with a creamy chardonnay.

# { If You've Got 40 Minutes }

TAMPERING WITH TRADITIONAL FARE

I sometimes—Ok, often—envy my friends who cook daring, exotic dishes and throw crazy things like fruit into veggie salads. Innovative stuff like that doesn't go over so well in my house. I can prepare it, but Hubby will stare down at the unfamiliar thing on his plate with suspicious distaste. He's a creature of habit, even more so a creature of tradition. Not only does he want to eat the *same* things, he wants them prepared in the most traditional way. To him, it's not really *Shabbos* without classic gefilte fish and chicken soup. And even when it's 99° outside—steaming hot chulent and potato kugel better be on the menu.

I want my kids to be ready to try new things and the best way
to do that is to expose them to all kinds of fare, so in this book—
and specifically in this chapter—I'm primed to tweak tradition.

Defending this bias with his favorite phrase "Well, that's how I had it growing up…," he will insist on chopped liver, even when there are a dozen other sides on the table. Garden salad should be served sans dressing, with multiple bottled dressings standing alongside the salad bowl cuz, "That's how I had it growing up…" (Never mind that when *I* was growing up, bottles on the table were worse than elbows.) Even the salad itself should be boring, made with iceberg lettuce. *Iceberg!* No colorful fruit slices, exotic greens, toasted nuts, or onions of any color except white in this nostalgic salad of his childhood.

Listen, I will gladly love and honor Hubby forever, but I go off when he begs for gefilte fish out of a jar. Granted, he prefers my more or less "homemade" version—as long as it's plated exactly the same way as it was when he was growing up—but those jellied fishballs are his unerring default. To tell the truth, I developed my own addiction to the taste—especially to the jelly itself—but eventually it seemed just too easy. Our grandmothers used to spend a whole day making gefilte fish from scratch—and that included cleaning the fish, gutting it, boning it, and chopping it in a wooden bowl. How can I get away with just opening a jar? Yet when I was a new bride—and all thumbs in the kitchen—I stocked up on this wondrous stuff, knowing that it could last unrefrigerated in my pantry until our 50th wedding anniversary. When guests would visit, Hubby would say, "You have to see this," and show off our cupboard filled like an aquarium with jars of gefilte fish. Go figure.

But when I finally learned to cook, I got restless. More than restless: I got daring. I wanna try new tastes, new ingredients, unusual combinations. I want my kids to be gustatorily gutsy too, not addicted to familiar foods like a certain spouse I happen to know. I want them to be ready to try new things, and the best way to do that is to expose them to all kinds of fare. So in this book, I'm primed to tamper with tradition.

And it doesn't have to take long to prepare either. I've already done all the legwork— wandered the virtual globe for you—searching out genuine ethnic influences that will add something exotic to your table in just **40 minutes flat**! Think of it—in just over a half hour, you can take your family on a culinary magic carpet ride to Ireland or Vietnam, France or Scandinavia— anywhere but Philadelphia.

Yes, dear reader, *you* are my excuse to try out funky foods! Whenever I want to prepare something exciting, I tell Hubby I'm recipe-testing for the book. It's not that he won't eat it: he'll dutifully down the new cuisine with a smile on his face and even say something encouraging, like, "People out there will LOVE this!" But he's not fooling me. I know he'd rather be downing his Mama's tried-and-true pot roast.

Sometimes I sweetly promise him that I'll stick to something "traditional." Then I bring out my Potato, Corn, and Cod Chowder, complete with biscuits and iceberg lettuce salad. Hey, it's traditional in New England! And I knew he'd go for the salad—with the iceberg lettuce and all. When I brought out the Lamb Koftkas—lamb meatballs nestled in pita bread—Hubby protested that this couldn't possibly be "traditional." Is too—if you live in North Africa.

# If you can wrap your taste buds around foods from the Far East, you'll discover the amazing sensations you get from Summer Rolls

Sometimes I'll zap him with more "traditional" fare—and I don't mean brisket. There are other places in the world, m'dear, like Mexico or Asia, where traditions have a flavor all their own. These were never known to *shtetl* Jews, but our global generation has adopted them and learned to love their exotic tang. (Of course, Sephardic Jews have a jump on this because they're accustomed to "traditional" dishes popping with spices.) Whoever said that Black Bean Burritos and Chicken Fiesta are not Jewish foods? They are! In Guadalajara. And if you can wrap your taste buds around foods from the Far East, you'll discover the amazing sensations you get from my Thai Chicken Soup (flavored with coconut milk, cilantro, and lime juice) and Summer Rolls made from rice paper wraps. Miso-Glazed Salmon is commonplace in Japan, but when it hit the kosher restaurants in the U.S., it was a totally new treat. Now it's almost an old fashioned Jewish food, like sushi. What's a Bar Mitzvah smorg without sushi? Hey, these days you can't shop at any supermarket worth its weight in kosher salt without being able to pick up a sushi roll.

You think our brothers and sisters in Hong Kong have been sitting around eating *knaidlach*? Well, ok, maybe they have—but we can still learn a thing or two from the cooks in the countryside around them.

Even though these dishes sound fancy, I will show you how to make them in less time than it takes to do a load of laundry, whether you are in Kansas City, Kalamazoo, or Kyoto.

I concede that there's also indispensable mainstream chow and I never put it down, because —like most Americans—I was raised on the stuff and it's in my bones (and, of course, that's how Hubby had it when he was growing up.) But I want to show you some daring, uncommon combinations, some familiar foods prepared in a fresh new way and a kosher approach to traditionally non-kosher dishes.

So let's have some fun. Here are recipes that are traditional *somewhere,* or start out as conventional fare—and end up with a few surprises!

{40} minute meals

# { Aromatic Baked Flounder over Capellini }

**Serves 4** | Put up water to boil for the capellini before you start making the flounder.

## Aromatic Baked Flounder over Capellini

1 onion, halved lengthwise and thinly sliced

2 shallots, thinly sliced

1 leek, halved lengthwise, rinsed, dried, and thinly sliced

1 tablespoon olive oil

½ teaspoon dried thyme or 1 ½ teaspoons fresh

1 teaspoon kosher salt

½ teaspoon cracked black pepper

4 flounder filets, about 1 ½ pounds

2 cloves garlic, minced

1 cup canned diced tomatoes, undrained

2 tablespoons orange zest

½ pound capellini

Preheat oven to 425° F.

Place onions, shallots, and leeks in an 11- x 14-inch baking dish. Toss together with olive oil, thyme, salt, and pepper. Lay flounder on top of vegetables.

In a small bowl, mix garlic, tomatoes, and orange zest, and pour over flounder.

Bake for 15 minutes.

Prepare capellini according to package instructions. Place on a serving platter.

Serve flounder over the bed of capellini.

## Flounder Facts

*Flounder are known for their firm texture and delicate sweet flavor. Founder is lean fish, so it is not suitable for stir-frying or grilling and can dry out if overcooked. Capellini, also called angel hair, is a perfect complement for flounder; it's a very thin pasta that cooks quickly.*

**Recommended Wine:
Yatir Sauvignon Blanc**

Flounder is a delicate and flaky fish which requires a wine that will not overpower its subtle flavors and texture. Try a crisp and refreshing sauvignon blanc.

# {BBQ Pulled Chicken Sandwiches}
## Collard Greens

**Serves 4** | First prepare Collard Greens. While they are cooking, move on to the chicken sandwiches.

## BBQ Pulled Chicken Sandwiches

*At Kosher.com, we have the perfect BBQ roasted chicken—courtesy of Chap-a-nosh, a family catering business that's been around almost as long as I have.*

**3** to 4 cups rotisserie chicken, about a 3-pound chicken, skin removed

**2** cups barbeque sauce

**4** kaiser rolls, split in half

**1** avocado, pitted, peeled, and sliced

Using your fingers or two forks, pull chicken from the bones, shredding it into medium strands.

Combine chicken and barbeque sauce in a medium saucepan. Cook over medium heat, stirring occasionally, for about 10 minutes, or until chicken is heated through.

Arrange 4 roll halves on a serving platter. Evenly distribute chicken among the rolls. Top with avocado slices, then the roll tops, and serve with Collard Greens.

## Collard Greens

*See note about Worcestershire sauce, page 245.*

**2** tablespoons canola oil

**½** medium onion, coarsely chopped

**1** bunch collard greens, rinsed, stems removed, and finely chopped

**1** tablespoon kosher salt

**¼** cup Manischewitz Reduced Sodium All Natural Chicken Broth

**1** teaspoon Worcestershire sauce

Heat oil over medium heat in a 12-inch skillet. Add onions, collards, salt, broth, and Worcestershire sauce; mix well. Cook, uncovered, stirring occasionally for 25 minutes, or until tender.

## Avocado Tricks

*Pit, peel, and slice avocados just before serving so they don't brown. Squeezing fresh lemon juice over avocados will slow oxidization.*

**Recommended Wine:**
**Cuvée Du Centenaire (Cotes du Rhóne)**

The saucy shredded chicken will go nicely with a full-bodied red wine. Find a red that is fruity or even jammy—this will pair nicely with a sweet BBQ sauce.

# { Beef Sausage and Pepper Rolls }
## Fresh Mint Lemonade

. . . . . . . . . . . . . . . . . . . . . . . . . . . . . . . . . . . . . . . . . . . . . . . . . . . . . . . . . . . . . . . . . . . . . . . . . . . . . . . .

**Serves 4** | While sausage and peppers are cooking, prepare lemonade.

## Beef Sausage and Pepper Rolls

*There are many different terms for this type of sandwich depending on which region of the United States a person is from: submarine or sub, hoagie, hero, grinder, bomber, torpedo, poorboy, blimpie, and wedge. Serve with watermelon slices for a refreshing contrast to the heaviness of the sausages and peppers.*

2   tablespoons canola oil

4   beef sausages

1   red pepper

1   green pepper

1   yellow pepper

1   large onion

2   tablespoons Bartenura Balsamic Vinegar

    Kosher salt

    Freshly ground black pepper

4   grinder (or sub) rolls, halved horizontally

Heat canola oil in a large sauté pan over medium heat. Brown sausages, turning often to cook evenly, about 8 minutes. When sausages plump up, pierce them with a fork to release their juices.

While sausages are browning, prepare peppers and onion: Cut peppers lengthwise; remove stems and seeds, and slice into ¼-inch strips. Peel and cut onion in half lengthwise, and slice into ¼-inch strips.

Add onions and peppers to sausages in pan. Stir to combine. Cover and cook for 5 minutes. Remove cover; add balsamic vinegar and stir. Continue cooking over medium heat for 7 to 8 minutes. Season with salt and pepper to taste.

To prepare rolls: Separate halves and place them in a toaster oven or under the broiler for 30 to 60 seconds, keeping an eye on them so they don't burn.

Distribute the sausages and peppers evenly among the toasted rolls. Serve with Fresh Mint Lemonade and watermelon slices.

## Fresh Mint Lemonade

*The trick to making good lemonade is to use a simple syrup which is made with equal parts water and sugar. Simple syrup can be used for the base of many drinks, including sangria.*

1   cup sugar

4   cups cold water, divided

1   cup freshly squeezed lemon juice

3   sprigs fresh mint

In a small saucepan over medium heat, mix sugar with 1 cup water. Cook until sugar dissolves, stirring continually, for 3 to 5 minutes.

Pour the sugar syrup, lemon juice, and remaining 3 cups water into a pitcher; add mint and stir well.

Serve in tall glasses over ice.

. . . . . . . . . . . . . . . . . . . . . . . . . . . . . . . . . . . . . . . . . . . . . . .

**Recommended Wine:**
**Weinstock "Red by W"**

Sausages and their associated spice can be uncomfortable when intensified by a tannic red wine. Try this dish with a young red wine with low tannins.

# { Black Bean Burritos with Ancho Chile Rice }

**Serves 4** | While beans are cooking, prepare rice and begin peppers.

## Black Bean Burritos with Ancho Chile Rice

*In this recipe, we are using both the cilantro stems and leaves: the stems in the beans and the leaves in the burritos.*

For beans:

- 1 tablespoon canola oil
- ½ medium onion, finely chopped
- 1 (15 ½-ounce) can black beans, rinsed and drained
- 1 teaspoon ground cumin
- 1 tablespoon finely chopped fresh cilantro stems
- ½ teaspoon kosher salt
- 1 cup Manischewitz All Natural Vegetable Broth

For rice:

- 1 cup instant rice
  Manischewitz All Natural Vegetable Broth
- 1 teaspoon ancho chili powder

For peppers:

- 3 poblano peppers
  Olive oil

For assembly:

- 4 (8-inch) tortillas, any variety
- 2 cups Les Petites Fermieres Shredded Cheddar
- 2 medium tomatoes, coarsely chopped
- 4 tablespoons torn fresh cilantro leaves
- 1 (16-ounce) container regular or low-fat sour cream
- 1 (8-ounce) container guacamole
- 1 (12-ounce) jar mild salsa

To prepare black beans:
Heat oil in a large sauté pan over medium heat. Add onions and cook for 8 minutes. Add black beans, cumin, cilantro stems, salt, and broth; mix well. Cover and let cook for 15 minutes over medium heat, until most of the broth is absorbed. Mash beans with a potato masher.

To prepare rice:
Prepare according to package instructions, substituting vegetable broth for water and adding chili powder.

To roast peppers:
Oil peppers and place them on a baking sheet. Broil peppers, turning often with tongs to char on all sides. Once they are charred, place peppers in a paper bag. Shake peppers in the bag to remove most of the char. Let peppers sit in the closed bag for 10 minutes. Remove peppers from the bag and dry with paper towels. Seed peppers and cut in strips.

To assemble:
Place tortillas on a plate, covered with a damp paper towel. Heat in the microwave for 20 seconds. Lay tortillas out on a work surface.

Evenly distribute the black bean mixture among the tortillas, leaving 2 inches around the perimeter. Layer cheese, poblano strips, tomatoes, cilantro leaves, and rice on top of the beans.

To make burritos: Fold in the sides to meet in the middle; then roll up the burrito, starting from the bottom. Cut burritos in half and place, seam-side down, on dinner plates. Serve with sour cream, guacamole, and salsa in small bowls on the side.

**Recommended Wine:**
**Capcanes Peraj Petita
(Tempranillo/Grenache blend)**

This Mexican-inspired dish can handle a red wine, but go for one that is medium in body with good fruit and acidity.

# { Blueberry and Lemon Pancakes }
## Blueberry Maple Syrup

. . . . . . . . . . . . . . . . . . . . . . . . . . . . . . . . . . . . . . . . . . . . . . . . . . . . . . . . . . . . . . . . . . . . . . .

**Serves 4** | Yield 12 Pancakes

## Blueberry and Lemon Pancakes

*This is a total blueberry blast! A fun and yummy recipe for both children and adults. Serve it just like they do at restaurants with coffee, tea, and orange juice or milk.*

2   **cups flour**

2   **tablespoons sugar**

1   **tablespoon baking powder**

½   **teaspoon baking soda**

½   **teaspoon salt**

4   **tablespoons butter, melted, at room temperature**

1   **large egg**

1   **½ cups whole milk**

   **Zest of 1 lemon**

2   **cups blueberries, rinsed and dried**

   **Canola oil**

   **Sour cream**

In a mixing bowl, whisk together flour, sugar, baking powder, baking soda, and salt. In a small bowl, whisk together melted butter, egg, and milk.

Just before cooking the pancakes, stir the egg mixture into the flour mixture and gently fold in lemon zest and blueberries.

Heat a lightly oiled large nonstick skillet or griddle over medium heat until hot. Ladle ¼ cup pancake batter in pools, about 1 inch apart. Cook for about 5 minutes until bubbles appear on the tops of the pancakes. Gently flip over and continue cooking until golden on the bottom, about 2 to 3 minutes.

Serve with sour cream and Blueberry Maple Syrup.

## Blueberry Maple Syrup

1   **cup maple syrup**

½   **cup blueberries, rinsed and dried**

In a small saucepan over low heat, combine maple syrup and blueberries. Cook for 10 minutes, stirring. Maple syrup can burn very quickly so watch it carefully. Pour into a small pitcher for serving.

. . . . . . . . . . . . . . . . . . . . . . . . . . . . . . . . . . . . . .

**Recommended Wine:**
**Jeunesse Cabernet Sauvignon**

Though pancakes are considered to be a breakfast dish, adding a slightly sweet red wine with berry characteristics will complete the meal and make it dinner worthy!

# { Blueberry Cheese Quesadillas }
## Sweet Potato Leek Soup

**Serves 4** | Cook soup first. While the soup is simmering, prepare Blueberry and Cheese Quesadillas.

## Blueberry Cheese Quesadillas

*Chèvre is French for goat cheese.*

- I cup fresh blueberries, rinsed and dried
- I peach, pitted, peeled and cut in wedges
- I cup Natural & Kosher Natural Chèvre, crumbled
- ½ medium red onion, finely chopped
- I teaspoon fresh thyme leaves
- 4 (8-inch) flour tortillas
- Gefen Canola Oil Cooking Spray

Mix blueberries, peaches, goat cheese, onions, and thyme in a medium bowl.

Lay out tortillas on a work surface. Spoon one-quarter blueberry filling over half of each tortilla. Fold the other half of the tortilla over filling.

Spray a large sauté pan with cooking spray. Heat the pan over medium heat until hot. Place two quesadillas, side by side, in the pan. Cook for 2 minutes on each side or until cheese is melted, being careful not to burn. Transfer quesadillas to a cutting board. Cook remaining two quesadillas. Cut each quesadilla into three wedges.

Plate quesadillas and serve with Sweet Potato Leek Soup.

## Sweet Potato Leek Soup

*Sweating is a cooking technique by which vegetables are cooked in a small amount of fat over low heat. The vegetables cook in their own juices and soften but do not brown.*

- 2 tablespoons canola oil
- I medium onion, finely chopped
- I clove garlic, minced
- 2 leeks, white and light green parts, rinsed, dried, and thinly sliced
- 2 sweet potatoes, peeled and cut in ¼-inch cubes
- I tablespoon kosher salt
- ½ teaspoon cayenne pepper
- I (32-ounce) box Manischewitz All Natural Vegetable Broth
- ¼ cup chopped fresh flat leaf parsley

Heat oil in a stockpot over medium-high heat. Add onions, garlic, and leeks. Sweat vegetables for 5 minutes. Add sweet potatoes, salt, and cayenne; mix well. Cook for 5 minutes more. Stir in broth and parsley. Cover and bring to a boil; reduce heat, and simmer for 15 minutes. Adjust seasoning, if needed.

**Recommended Wine:**
**Segal's "Fusion" Red (blend)**

The cheesy quesadillas and rich sweet potato soup will pair nicely with a full-bodied white wine or a medium-bodied red.

# { Cheese Fondue }
## Chocolate Fondue

. . . . . . . . . . . . . . . . . . . . . . . . . . . . . . . . . . . . . . . . . . . . . . . . . . . . . . . .

**Serves 8** | This is a nontraditional meal. You will be serving the sweet and savory fondues side by side. A fondue supper is a wonderful way for the whole family to enjoy creating and eating a meal together.

## Cheese Fondue

*Fondue pots are essential to the success of this meal. A proper pot will keep your fondue warm and the perfect consistency right at your tabletop.*

2   tablespoons flour

1   tablespoon mustard powder

1   teaspoon freshly ground black pepper

1   tablespoon butter

2   cups whole milk

2   tablespoons Worcestershire sauce

1   frozen cube Gefen Crushed Garlic

2   tablespoons white wine

2   cups Les Petites Fermieres Shredded Cheddar

2   cups Les Petites Fermieres Gouda, shredded

2   cups Natural & Kosher Shredded Mozzarella

1   loaf French bread, cut into chunks

    Fresh or steamed vegetables of your choice

Whisk together flour, mustard, and pepper.

In a medium saucepan over low heat, melt butter. Whisk in flour mixture; continuing to whisk until mixture (roux) is smooth, about 4 minutes. Flour will start to "honeycomb" when done.

Combine milk, Worcestershire sauce, and garlic in a small bowl.

Gradually whisk wine into roux, then gradually whisk in milk mixture, allowing the roux to absorb the liquid before adding more. If you add the liquid too quickly, the flour will clump.

Let sauce come to a slow boil, about 5 minutes; reduce heat to low. Stirring often, cook for 8 minutes or until sauce is thickened and can coat a wooden spoon. Add cheeses and cook until melted, about 1 to 2 minutes.

Pour into a fondue pot over a low flame and serve with a platter of bread and vegetables.

## Chocolate Fondue

*Cubed brownies, chocolate chip cookies, and dried fruits are all great dipping treats.*

2   (16-ounce) bags semisweet chocolate chips

2   cups heavy cream

2   teaspoons vanilla extract

    Strawberries, rinsed, hulled, and dried

    Bananas, sliced

    Marshmallows

    Store-bought pound cake, in 1-inch cubes

Place chocolate chips in a fondue pot. In a small saucepan over low heat, heat cream to a low simmer, being careful not to boil. Pour cream over chocolate chips, add vanilla, and stir until chips are melted.

Serve in the fondue pot, over a low flame, with a platter of fruit, marshmallows, and cake.

. . . . . . . . . . . . . . . . . . . . . . . . . . . . . . . . . . . . . . . .

**Recommended Wine:**
**Porto Cordovero**

Soft or melted cheese can, at times, clash with red wine; while sweets such as chocolate can make red wine taste bitter. Go for a dessert wine here—or even a port!

# { Cheese Soufflé }
## Simple Green Salad

**Serves 2** | While the soufflé is baking, prepare salad greens and dressing; toss together just before serving.

## Cheese Soufflé

*Once cooked, the soufflé deflates quickly so be ready to serve immediately.*

> **Butter for greasing soufflé dish**
2 **tablespoons Natural & Kosher Grated Parmesan**
½ **cup whole milk**
1 **tablespoon butter**
1 **tablespoon flour**
¼ **teaspoon kosher salt**
¼ **teaspoon mustard powder**
> **Pinch ground nutmeg**
1 **large egg yolk**
2 **large egg whites**
¼ **cup Natural & Kosher Sliced Swiss, finely chopped or grated**

Preheat oven to 400° F. Move rack to the lowest third of the oven. Butter 2 (6- or 8-ounce) soufflé dishes. Dust each dish with 1 tablespoon Parmesan, making sure that the sides and bottom are well coated. Set aside.

Microwave milk for 30 seconds.

In a medium saucepan over medium-low heat, melt butter. Whisk in flour, whisking continually for 2 minutes, being careful not to let the mixture burn.

Add warm milk in a steady stream and whisk continually for about 3 minutes until thickened. Mixture should coat the back of a wooden spoon when thick. Whisk in the salt, mustard, and nutmeg. Remove from heat.

In a small bowl, beat egg yolk. Temper yolk by whisking in a little butter sauce. Slowly whisk tempered egg yolk into the rest of the sauce. Set aside.

In a large bowl, with an electric mixer, beat egg whites until stiff, about 5 minutes. Fold about half of the beaten egg whites into the sauce. Sprinkle half of the cheese into the sauce. Fold in remaining egg whites and then remaining cheese.

Divide batter equally between the prepared dishes. Place them on a baking pan large enough to hold both dishes. Bake for about 16 minutes. Do not open the oven door during baking; opening the door can cause the soufflé to fall. Use the oven light to check on the soufflé; when the soufflé has puffed, it is done.

Serve with Simple Green Salad.

## Simple Green Salad

> 2 **cups packaged salad greens, rinsed and dried**
¼ **cup Basic Vinaigrette (see recipe page 43)**

In a large bowl, toss salad greens with vinaigrette and serve.

**Recommended Wine:**
**Gamla Chardonnay**

This light and creamy dish will go very nicely with a medium-bodied white wine, especially one with a creamy texture like a chardonnay.

# { Chicken Fiesta }

**Serves 4**

## Chicken Fiesta

*This recipe uses a Mexican-inspired rub for the chicken fingers. Making a rub, which is a mixture of spices to be applied to meat, fish, and poultry, is very easy to do and takes no time at all. Making your own also guarantees that your family won't be eating unpronounceable fillers.*

| | |
|---|---|
| 1 | **teaspoon ground cumin** |
| 1 | **teaspoon paprika** |
| 2 | **teaspoons kosher salt** |
| ¼ | **teaspoon garlic powder** |
| ¼ | **teaspoon onion powder** |
| ¼ | **teaspoon chili powder** |
| 1 | **pound boneless, skinless chicken breast, cut in 3-inch strips** |
| 1 | **mango, pitted and peeled** |
| 1 | **avocado, pitted and peeled** |
| 1 | **red pepper, ribs and seeds removed** |
| 2 | **scallions** |
| 1 | **large red onion** |
| ¼ | **cup freshly squeezed lime juice** |
| ¼ | **cup honey** |
| 2 | **tablespoons olive oil** |
| 3 | **tablespoons canola oil** |
| 8 | **(8-inch) whole wheat tortillas** |
| 8 | **leaves Bibb lettuce, rinsed and dried** |

To make rub: In small bowl, combine cumin, paprika, salt, garlic powder, onion powder, and chili powder. Rub over chicken fingers and set aside for 10 minutes.

While chicken is resting: Cut mango and avocado into 1-inch cubes. Slice pepper into strips. Thinly slice scallions diagonally. Halve onion lengthwise and thinly slice.

In a medium bowl, combine lime juice, honey, and olive oil. Mix in mango, avocado, peppers, scallions, and onions.

In a large sauté pan, heat canola oil over medium-high heat. Add chicken fingers and sauté for 10 minutes, or until thoroughly cooked.

Place tortillas on a microwavable plate, cover with a damp paper towel, and heat for 30 to 60 seconds.

To assemble tortillas: Lay out tortillas on a work surface. Place one lettuce leaf on one half of each tortilla. Evenly distribute chicken fingers and mango salad over the lettuce. Fold the other half of the tortilla over filling and serve with sweetened iced coffee or tea.

**Recommended Wine:**
**Elvi Matiz Rioja**

This Mexican inspired dish calls for a Latin pairing. Try a juicy Spanish Rioja.

# {Chicken Marsala}
## Garlic Mashed Potatoes

. . . . . . . . . . . . . . . . . . . . . . . . . . . . . . . . . . . . . . . . . . . . . . . . . . . . . . . . . . . . . . . . . . . . . . . . . . . . . . . . . . . . . .

Serves 4 | Start the Garlic Mashed Potatoes first. While the potatoes are cooking, prepare Chicken Marsala.

## Chicken Marsala

*You can use a mixture of button, shiitake, crimini, and baby bella mushrooms for this dish. Using a whisk to mix the flour with the seasonings guarantees an even blending. You might have to pound the chicken to get it to the correct thickness.*

1   cup flour
1   teaspoon dried thyme
1   teaspoon kosher salt
½   teaspoon freshly ground black pepper
4   tablespoons olive oil, divided
2   cups assorted thinly-sliced mushrooms
1 ½ pounds chicken cutlets, cut in ¼-inch strips
½   cup Marsala wine
¼   cup Manischewitz All Natural Chicken Broth

Combine flour, thyme, salt, and pepper in a shallow bowl.

In a 12-inch skillet, heat 2 tablespoons oil over medium-high heat. Add mushrooms and cook for 10 minutes. Transfer the mushrooms to a small bowl and set aside.

Heat remaining 2 tablespoons oil in the skillet. Dip chicken in flour mixture. Shake off excess flour and place chicken in hot oil. Do not crowd chicken or it will steam instead of brown. Cook for 5 minutes on each side. Transfer to a platter and cover with foil to keep warm.

Once all of the chicken has been cooked, add wine to the skillet, stirring up all of the browned bits and pieces. Increase heat to high and continue cooking for 2 minutes. Stir in broth, and cook for 3 minutes more or until sauce thickens. Return mushrooms to pan and heat through.

Pour sauce over chicken and serve with Garlic Mashed Potatoes.

## Garlic Mashed Potatoes

2   pounds Yukon gold potatoes, peeled and cut in small chunks
2   tablespoons kosher salt
2   cloves garlic, smashed
¼   to ½ cup Manischewitz All Natural Chicken Broth
4   tablespoons pareve margarine

Place potatoes, salt, and garlic in a 4-quart pot with enough water to cover the potatoes. Bring to a boil. Reduce heat to medium and cook until potatoes are fork tender, about 20 minutes.

Warm broth in a small saucepan over low heat.

Drain potatoes and place in a large bowl. Add broth and margarine and mash with a potato masher, electric mixer, or ricer to desired consistency.

. . . . . . . . . . . . . . . . . . . . . . . . . . . . . . . . . . . . . . . .

**Recommended Wine:**
**Barkan Reserve "Altitude Series—624" Cabernet Sauvignon**

Though chicken cutlets can, at times, be overwhelmed by a big red wine, the marsala wine and meaty mushrooms in this dish make it a heartier meal capable of handling a big-bodied red wine.

# { Chicken Paillard with Fried Sage }
## Angel Hair Al'olio | Sautéed Cherry Tomatoes

**Serves 4** | Keep chicken warm, covered in foil or in a warmed oven (with the heat off), while preparing the pasta. While pasta is cooking, sauté garlic and cook tomatoes.

## Chicken Paillard with Fried Sage

*Paillard is a term referring to a slice of meat pounded thin and quickly sautéed or grilled.*

½  **cup flour**
¼  **cup matzoh meal**
1  **tablespoon kosher salt**
1  **teaspoon freshly ground black pepper**
4  **(¼-inch thick) chicken cutlets, approximately 1 ½ pounds**
1  **large egg**
¼  **cup olive oil**
1  **bunch fresh sage leaves, rinsed and dried completely**
½  **cup Manischewitz All Natural Chicken Broth**

Preheat oven to 250° F.

Whisk flour and matzoh meal with salt and pepper in a shallow bowl. In a second shallow bowl, beat egg with 1 tablespoon water.

Dip chicken in egg, then coat with flour mixture. Place chicken pieces in a single layer on a plate, and set aside.

In a sauté pan large enough to hold all the chicken, heat oil over medium heat. When oil is hot, fry sage leaves for about 15 seconds until brown but not burnt. Remove and set aside.

Gently place chicken in oil and cook over high heat for 3 to 4 minutes on each side. Do not crowd chicken or it will steam instead of brown. When chicken is thoroughly cooked, transfer to a serving platter. Place platter in oven; turn off heat.

Drain oil from the pan. Add broth, stirring to get up all of the browned bits.

Remove platter from oven. Spoon broth over paillards (chicken) and garnish with fried sage leaves. Serve with Angel Hair Al'olio and Sautéed Cherry Tomatoes.

## Angel Hair Al'olio

½  **pound angel hair**
¾  **cup olive oil**
4  **cloves garlic, minced**
¼  **cup chopped fresh parsley**

Cook angel hair according to package instructions, drain, and place in a serving bowl.

While the pasta is cooking, heat oil in a small saucepan over low heat. Add garlic and gently cook for 3 minutes.

Toss angel hair with oil, garlic, and parsley.

## Sautéed Cherry Tomatoes

1  **pint cherry tomatoes, rinsed and dried**
1  **tablespoon olive oil**
1  **teaspoon Gefen Coarse Sea Salt**
½  **teaspoon cracked black pepper**

Heat oil in a small sauté pan over medium-high heat. When oil is hot, add tomatoes and stir quickly until skins pop. Transfer to a medium serving bowl; season with salt and pepper.

**Recommended Wine:**
**Segal's Chardonnay Special Reserve**

This delicately prepared chicken breast will pair very nicely with a complex white wine.

# { Chicken with Braised Red Cabbage and Fennel }

## Noodles with Poppy Seeds

........................................................

**Serves 4** | While chicken is cooking prepare Noodles with Poppy Seeds.

## Chicken with Braised Red Cabbage and Fennel

*Fennel is sometimes called anise.*

3   tablespoons canola oil

1   medium onion, coarsely chopped

1   (3-pound) chicken, cut in eighths

1   tablespoon kosher salt

1   teaspoon freshly ground black pepper

1   (10-ounce) bag shredded red cabbage, rinsed and dried

½   head fennel, shredded

2   cups Manischewitz All Natural Chicken Broth, more if necessary

1   teaspoon dried thyme

Applesauce (optional)

Heat oil in a large sauté pan over medium heat. Add onions and sauté them for 5 minutes or until soft.

Season chicken with salt and pepper. Add chicken to the pan and brown for about 8 minutes on each side. Transfer to a bowl.

Add cabbage, fennel, broth, and thyme to the pan, mixing well. Bring to a boil. Return chicken to the pan, reduce the heat to a high simmer. Cover and cook for 15 minutes.

Transfer to a serving platter. Serve with Noodles with Poppy Seeds and applesauce, if desired.

## Noodles with Poppy Seeds

1   (12-ounce) package extra wide egg noodles

3   tablespoons pareve margarine, melted

1   tablespoon poppy seeds

Cook noodles according to package instructions and drain well. Transfer to a serving bowl and toss well with margarine and poppy seeds.

........................................................

**Recommended Wine:
Barkan Barrel Aged Reserve Shiraz**

The red cabbage and rich chicken will hold up very nicely to a robust red wine, especially one that has aromas of fennel or anise such as a Shiraz.

# { Chicken with Prunes and Oregano }
## Baby Zucchini Sauté

. . . . . . . . . . . . . . . . . . . . . . . . . . . . . . . . . . . . . . . . . . . . . . . . . . . . . . . . . . . . . . . . . . . .

**Serves 4 to 6** | Prepare Baby Zucchini Sauté while chicken is baking.

## Chicken with Prunes and Oregano

6   chicken legs with thighs attached, about 4 pounds
1   tablespoon kosher salt
1   teaspoon freshly ground black pepper
¼   cup olive oil
¼   cup finely chopped shallots or red onion
3   cloves garlic, minced
¼   cup recommended red wine (see below)
1   cup pitted prunes
¼   cup capers, drained
1   bay leaf
2   tablespoons dried oregano
½   cup packed light brown sugar
½   cup **Manischewitz All Natural Chicken Broth**

Preheat oven to 350° F.

Season chicken legs with salt and pepper.

Heat olive oil over high heat in an ovenproof sauté pan or Dutch oven large enough to hold all of the ingredients. Brown chicken legs about 10 minutes, and transfer to a bowl. Add shallots and garlic to olive oil and cook for 2 minutes. Add red wine and continue cooking for 1 minute more. Add prunes, capers, bay leaf, and oregano; mix well. Cook for 2 minutes. Return chicken to pan and sprinkle brown sugar on top.

Pour chicken broth in the bottom of the pan. Bake, uncovered, for 20 minutes, or until the juices run clear when chicken is pierced with a fork. Remove and discard bay leaf.

Transfer chicken to a serving platter surrounded by prune mixture and Baby Zucchini Sauté.

## Baby Zucchini Sauté

2   tablespoons olive oil
1   shallot, minced
12  baby zucchini, halved lengthwise
1   teaspoon kosher salt
¼   teaspoon freshly ground black pepper

In a medium sauté pan, heat oil over medium heat; add shallots and cook for 1 minute.

Add zucchini and cook for 3 to 4 minutes, shaking the pan occasionally. Season with salt and pepper.

. . . . . . . . . . . . . . . . . . . . . . . . . . . . . . . . . . . . . . . . . .

**Recommended Wine:**
**Teal Lake Shiraz/Cabernet Sauvignon**

Red wine, prunes and dark meat chicken—the perfect recipe for a winter-time red!

# { Chicken, Pear, and Arugula Salad }
## Simple Butternut Squash Soup

......................................................................

**Serves 4**

## Chicken, Pear, and Arugula Salad

*I love Bosc pears. They are crisp, sweet, and spicy. They are wonderful salad pears and terrific for cooking and baking.*

- 1 **pound boneless, skinless chicken breasts, cut into strips**
- ¼ **cup Buffalo-style wing sauce**
- 2 **tablespoons canola oil**
- 2 **Bosc pears, unpeeled**
- 1 **lemon, halved**
- 1 **(5-ounce) package arugula, rinsed and dried**
- 1 **small red onion, halved lengthwise and thinly sliced**
- ½ **cup bottled raspberry vinaigrette, divided**
- 1 **cup store-bought candied walnuts**

In a medium bowl, toss chicken strips with wing sauce. In a large skillet, heat oil over medium heat. Cook chicken strips in the oil for 8 minutes, stirring occasionally.

While chicken is cooking, halve and core the pears and cut them into wedges. Squeeze lemon juice over pears to prevent browning.

In a large serving bowl, toss arugula and onions with ¼ cup raspberry vinaigrette.

Top with pear wedges, chicken strips, and walnuts. Serve remaining vinaigrette on the side.

Serve with Simple Butternut Squash Soup.

## Simple Butternut Squash Soup

*This soup is easy and quick to make using frozen squash and jarred applesauce which lend sweetness and richness to the soup. Winter squashes, like butternut, have a hard, inedible peel which is very difficult and time-consuming to remove. Now it is available peeled and cubed in packages in the produce section of many supermarkets. Using frozen squash also saves time.*

- 2 **tablespoons canola oil**
- 1 **medium onion, coarsely chopped**
- 1 **teaspoon dried thyme leaves**
- 1 **(12-ounce) package frozen puréed butternut squash, thawed**
- 1 **(2 ½-ounce) jar baby food applesauce or ⅓ cup regular applesauce**
- 1 **(32-ounce) box Manischewitz All Natural Chicken Broth**
- 2 **teaspoons kosher salt**
- 1 **teaspoon freshly ground black pepper**

Heat oil in a medium saucepan over medium heat. Add onions and cook for 5 minutes, stirring occasionally. Stir in thyme leaves, squash, applesauce, and chicken broth. Mix well and cook for 8 minutes. Add salt and pepper and stir. Remove from heat and let cool slightly.

With an immersion blender or food processor, purée soup for 3 to 5 minutes, or until smooth. Heat through and serve.

......................................................................

**Recommended Wine:
Carmel Ridge White**

Sweet and spicy meals such as these generally require a refreshing wine that can cleanse the palate with its acidity and tickle the tongue with a hint of sweetness.

# { Cranberry Walnut Salmon on a Bed of Spinach }

**Serves 8**

## Cranberry Walnut Salmon on a Bed of Spinach

*Do not spin or dry the spinach, the water that is on the leaves will provide the steam to cook it.*

For salmon:

- **Gefen Canola Oil Cooking Spray**
- 8 **(6-ounce) pieces salmon filet**
- 2 **tablespoons kosher salt**
- 1 **tablespoon paprika**
- 2 **teaspoons ground cumin**
- ½ **teaspoon ground cinnamon**
- **Pinch ground nutmeg**

For cranberry walnut topping:

- ½ **cup walnuts, coarsely chopped**
- 1 **tablespoon olive oil**
- 1 **small shallot, finely chopped**
- ½ **cup freshly squeezed orange juice**
- ¼ **cup honey**
- ½ **cup dried cranberries**
- ⅛ **teaspoon cayenne pepper**

For spinach:

- 2 **tablespoons olive oil**
- 4 **cloves garlic**
- 8 **(6-ounce) bags fresh baby spinach, rinsed and not dried**
- 2 **teaspoons lemon zest**
- 1 **tablespoon kosher salt**
- ¾ **teaspoon freshly ground black pepper**

Preheat oven to 375° F. Lightly spray a jelly-roll pan with cooking spray.

For salmon:
In a small bowl, mix together salt, paprika, cumin, cinnamon, and nutmeg. Rub spice mixture on each piece of salmon.

Place filets on prepared pan. Bake 15 to 20 minutes or until salmon is opaque and flakes easily with a fork.

For cranberry walnut topping:
Toast nuts in a small saucepan over medium heat for 5 minutes, stirring continually until lightly brown and fragrant. Remove from pan and set aside.

Heat oil in a small saucepan over medium heat. Add shallots and cook for 1 minute. Reduce heat to low. Add orange juice and honey; cook about 10 minutes or until sauce is thickened and syrupy. Add cranberries and cayenne pepper; stir until combined. Remove from heat, add nuts and pour over salmon.

For spinach:
Heat oil in a very large sauté pan over low heat. Add garlic and cook until fragrant, less than 1 minute. Add spinach to the pan. With tongs, toss spinach around as it wilts. Add lemon zest, salt, and pepper. Toss well.

Evenly distribute spinach among 8 dinner plates. Top each with 1 salmon filet. Spoon cranberry walnut topping over all.

**Recommended Wine:
Herzog Reserve Lodi Zinfandel**

Salmon is a fish that can handle red wine and the sweet and spicy nature of the cranberry sauce makes a rich and ripe American zinfandel a great pairing.

# { Creamy Mock Crab Salad Sandwiches }

## Oven-Roasted Balsamic Tomatoes

. . . . . . . . . . . . . . . . . . . . . . . . . . . . . . . . . . . . . . . . . . . . . . . .

**Serves 4** | Prepare the Oven-Roasted Balsamic Tomatoes first; and while they are in the oven, assemble the Creamy Mock Crab Salad Sandwiches.

## Creamy Mock Crab Salad Sandwiches

*This is also delicious on challah rolls, kaiser rolls, or your favorite sandwich bread.*

- 1 **pound imitation crabmeat**
- 1 **cup thinly sliced celery**
- ½ **cup finely chopped red onion**
- ¼ **cup chopped fresh dill**
- 1 **cup Gefen Regular or Lite Mayonnaise**
- ½ **cup capers, drained**
- 2 **tablespoons freshly squeezed lemon juice**
- 1 **teaspoon kosher salt**
- ¼ **teaspoon freshly ground black pepper**
- 4 **challah rolls, split**

In a large bowl, shred imitation crabmeat. Add celery, onions, dill, mayonnaise, capers, lemon juice, salt, and pepper. Gently toss together.

Toast rolls in toaster oven or under broiler or on grill.

Spoon salad onto rolls. Serve sandwiches on individual plates with Oven-Roasted Balsamic Tomatoes.

## Oven-Roasted Balsamic Tomatoes

- 4 **whole on-the-vine tomatoes**
  **Kosher salt**
  **Freshly ground black pepper**
- ¼ **cup Bartenura Balsamic Vinegar**

Preheat oven to 400° F. Line a jelly-roll pan with parchment paper.

Halve tomatoes and place on prepared pan, cut-side up. Season each half with salt and pepper to taste. Drizzle balsamic vinegar on top and roast for 25 minutes.

Remove from oven and transfer to a serving bowl.

. . . . . . . . . . . . . . . . . . . . . . . . . . . . . . . . . . . .

**Recommended Wine:
Herzog Reserve
Russian River Chardonnay**

The acid from the lemon juice combined with the creamy mayonnaise and toasted challah make this the perfect dish to pair with an oak-aged chardonnay.

# { Double Veggie Cheeseburgers }
## Corn on the Cob with Chili Lime Butter

. . . . . . . . . . . . . . . . . . . . . . . . . . . . . . . . . . . . . . . . . . . . . . . . . . . . . . . . . . . . . . . . . .

**Serves 4** | Prepare corn while veggie burgers are cooking.

## Double Veggie Cheeseburgers

8   frozen veggie burgers

4   hamburger buns, split in half

4   slices Natural & Kosher Mozzarella

4   slices Natural & Kosher Swiss

1   medium red onion, sliced

1   avocado, pitted, peeled, and sliced

2   medium ripe tomatoes, sliced

4   lettuce leaves

    Mustard

    Ketchup

Cook veggie burgers according to package instructions. In the last two minutes of cooking, place mozzarella cheese on 4 of the burgers and Swiss cheese on the other 4; allow cheese to melt.

Toast buns, if desired. Place 1 mozzarella burger on a bun. Place a Swiss burger on top of the mozzarella burger and the other bun half on top.

Place the burgers and fixins'— onions, avocados, tomatoes, lettuce, mustard, and ketchup— on a platter and serve with Corn on the Cob with Chili Lime Butter.

## Corn on the Cob with Chili Lime Butter

*A great way to serve corn is with flavored butters.*

4   ears of corn, shucked

4   tablespoons butter or pareve margarine

2   tablespoons freshly squeezed lime juice

1   teaspoon chili powder

1   teaspoon kosher salt

Fill a large pot three-quarters of the way to the top with water. Bring the water to a rolling boil. Add corn and boil for no more than 5 minutes.

While corn is cooking, melt butter in a small saucepan over low heat. Whisk in lime juice, chili powder, and salt. Remove from heat.

With tongs, transfer corn to a serving platter and brush with Chili Lime Butter.

. . . . . . . . . . . . . . . . . . . . . . . . . . . . . . . . . . . . . . .

**Recommended Wine:**
**Jeunesse Reserve Pinot Noir**

These cheesy veggie burgers would be overpowered by a robust red, but can be nicely complemented by a lighter pinot noir, maybe even one with a touch of sweetness.

# { Fish and "Chips" Sandwiches }
## Red and Green Coleslaw

Serves 4 | Prepare coleslaw first so the Fish and "Chips" Sandwiches can be served warm.

## Fish and "Chips" Sandwiches

*Deep frying can be very intimidating; but once you get the hang of it, it becomes another wonderful cooking technique in your repertoire. Cast iron pans work well. The oil needs to be only about 1-inch deep. Be careful not to let water come in contact with the hot oil—it will splatter and can burn you. If you do not have a deep fry thermometer, you can toss a 1-inch bread cube into the oil to determine if the oil is hot enough. If the bread browns in 30 seconds, the oil is ready.*

  Canola oil for deep frying
1 ½ pounds flounder or tilapia filet, cut in 3-inch pieces
1 cup flour
½ cup matzoh meal
1 tablespoon kosher salt
1 teaspoon cayenne pepper
2 large eggs, beaten
1 (12-ounce) can dark beer
4 hamburger buns, split in half
  Potato chips or vegetable chips
1 lemon, cut in 4 wedges

Pour 1-inch oil in a large heavy-bottomed pan. Heat over medium heat to 375° F. Lay out paper towels on a work surface.

To prepare batter: In a large bowl, whisk together flour, matzoh meal, salt, cayenne, eggs, and beer until smooth.

Coat fish with batter and let fish sit in batter while oil is heating.

When oil reaches desired temperature, gently place fish into pan. Cook for 4 minutes on each side. Fish should be well browned and crisp. Do not crowd fish in the pan; you may need to work in batches.

Remove fish from oil. Drain on paper towels and place on buns. Serve with chips, lemon wedges, and Red and Green Coleslaw on the side.

## Red and Green Coleslaw

2 cups packaged coleslaw mix
1 cup packaged shredded red cabbage
1 small red onion, finely chopped
½ cup packaged shredded carrots
1 cup Gefen Regular or Lite Mayonnaise
½ cup pickle relish
1 teaspoon sugar
2 tablespoons apple cider vinegar
1 teaspoon kosher salt
½ teaspoon freshly ground black pepper

In a salad bowl, mix coleslaw, cabbage, onions, and carrots together. In a small bowl, whisk mayonnaise, relish, sugar, vinegar, salt, and pepper. Toss the dressing with the slaw.

**Recommended Wine:**
**Binyamina Reserve Sauvignon Blanc**

Fried fish and coleslaw are dishes that can be difficult to pair with wine. The best solution when faced with difficult-to-pair dishes is to choose a refreshing (high acid) white wine which acts as a palate cleanser.

# { Ginger Chicken with Broccoli }

**Serves 4**

## Ginger Chicken with Broccoli

1  **tablespoon mustard powder**
1  **teaspoon ground ginger**
2  **teaspoons garlic powder**
4  **boneless chicken cutlets, cut in ¼-inch strips**
1  **cup frozen broccoli florets, thawed and drained**
¼  **cup soy sauce**
1  **(14-ounce) box instant rice**
   **Red pepper flakes (optional)**

Preheat oven to 375° F. Lay out 4 (18-inch) pieces of foil on your work surface.

In a large bowl, mix mustard, ginger, and garlic together; toss with chicken strips and broccoli.

Evenly distribute chicken and broccoli among the four pieces of foil. Pour 1 tablespoon soy sauce over each.

Fold the foil up to make a tent, leaving air space around the food. Crimp the edges well so the packet is well sealed. Bake for 15 minutes.

While chicken is baking, cook rice according to package instructions and set aside.

Spoon rice onto a serving platter. Open the foil packets and place chicken and broccoli over rice. Sprinkle with red pepper flakes, if desired.

## Foil Cooking

*To reduce the effects of the oven's direct heat (and your pile of dirty dishes), use aluminum foil. Place the food on the dull side of a large piece of foil. Wrap the foil up and around the food to create a tent. This tent will aid in heat circulation. Exposing the shiny side of the foil will further reflect the heat, keeping your food nice and moist.*

**Recommended Wine:
Capcanes Peraj Petita**

Strong flavors such as mustard, ginger, and garlic call for a lively and fruity wine with minerality.

# { Gourmet Egg Salad on Pumpernickel Toast Points }
## Rice Pudding

. . . . . . . . . . . . . . . . . . . . . . . . . . . . . . . . . . . . . . . . . . .

**Serves 6** | Prepare the Rice Pudding while the eggs are cooking.

## Gourmet Egg Salad on Pumpernickel Toast Points

*Assembling individual toast points can be time consuming. For a shortcut, try serving each person about 1 cup of egg salad on a bed of 1 to 2 large lettuce leaves with toast points on the side.*

8 **large eggs**

9 **slices pumpernickel bread**

½ **cup finely chopped celery**

¼ **cup finely chopped red onion**

¼ **to** ½ **cup Gefen Regular or Lite Mayonnaise**

1 **tablespoon kosher salt**

½ **teaspoon freshly ground black pepper**

¼ **teaspoon curry powder**

1 **teaspoon Dijon mustard**

1 **heart of romaine lettuce, washed, dried, and torn into bite-size pieces**

Preheat oven to 375° F.

To hard cook eggs: Place eggs in a medium saucepan with enough cold water to cover the eggs by 1 inch. Bring to a boil. Cover the pan and remove from the heat. Let stand for 14 minutes.

While eggs are cooking, trim crusts from bread to make a square. Stack bread and cut diagonally into quarters. Place bread on two jelly-roll pans. Toast in oven for about 5 minutes or until warm and crisp. Transfer toast points to a serving platter.

Pour off water from eggs, shake pan back and forth to break the shells. Fill pot with cold water and peel eggs under cold running water.

In a medium bowl, mash eggs with a fork. Add celery, onions, mayonnaise, salt, pepper, curry powder, and mustard; mix well. Top each toast point with lettuce and egg salad.

Serve with Rice Pudding for dessert.

## Rice Pudding

1 **cup whole milk**

**Pinch ground nutmeg**

1 **cup uncooked instant rice**

1 **(16-ounce) container vanilla yogurt**

½ **cup raisins (optional)**

**Cinnamon for dusting**

In a medium saucepan over medium-low heat, bring milk and nutmeg just to a boil, being careful not to let milk burn. Stir in rice. Remove from heat. Let stand, covered, for 5 minutes. Place rice mixture in a large bowl to cool, about 5 minutes. Add yogurt and raisins; mix well. Divide equally into 6 dessert cups. Sprinkle cinnamon on top of puddings.

. . . . . . . . . . . . . . . . . . . . . . . . . . . .

**Recommended Wine:**
**Bartenura Prosecco Brut**

A nice accompaniment to the Gourmet Egg Salad could be a classic mimosa. Mix equal parts orange juice and sparkling wine for a delicious brunch spritzer.

# { Grilled Salmon Caesar Salad }
## Homemade Croutons

. . . . . . . . . . . . . . . . . . . . . . . . . . . . . . . . . . . . . . . . . . . . . . . . . . . . . . . . . . . . . .

**Serves 4** | While the salmon is cooking, prepare the dressing and croutons.

## Grilled Salmon Caesar Salad

*Caesar salad was invented by Caesar Cardini at his restaurant in Tijuana, Mexico, on July 4, 1924. It was a busy weekend and he used ingredients on hand. Traditionally, a Caesar salad calls for a raw egg as a stabilizer and anchovies for flavor and saltiness. This recipe uses mayonnaise in place of the raw eggs and anchovy paste to save time. The anchovy paste is, of course, optional.*

> **Gefen Canola Oil Cooking Spray**
> 1 **½ to 2 pound salmon filet, cut into 4 pieces**
> **Kosher salt**
> **Freshly ground black pepper**
> 1 **cup Gefen Regular or Lite Mayonnaise**
> 2 **tablespoons freshly squeezed lemon juice**
> 1 **tablespoon Worcestershire sauce**
> 2 **cloves garlic, minced**
> 1 **teaspoon anchovy paste**
> 2 **tablespoons whole or low-fat milk**
> 2 **hearts of romaine lettuce, rinsed and dried, torn into bite-size pieces**
> 1 **cup Natural & Kosher Grated Parmesan**

Spray a grill pan with cooking spray and place over high heat. Season salmon with salt and pepper to taste. When pan is very hot, grill salmon for 5 to 6 minutes on each side, or until fish flakes easily with a fork.

Prepare dressing: In a blender or food processor, blend mayonnaise, lemon juice, Worcestershire sauce, garlic, anchovy paste, and milk until smooth.

Place greens, cheese, and croutons in a large bowl. Toss with ½ cup dressing.

Divide salad among 4 plates and place a piece of salmon on top of each salad.

Serve with Homeade Croutons and additional dressing on the side.

## Homemade Croutons

*To jazz up the croutons, try tossing the bread cubes with ¼ cup olive oil, 1 clove minced garlic, ¼ teaspoon dried thyme, ¼ teaspoon dried basil, ¼ teaspoon red pepper flakes, kosher salt and freshly ground black pepper to taste.*

> **Gefen Canola Oil Cooking Spray**
> 1 **loaf day-old bread, cut or torn into 3/4- to 1-inch square pieces**

Preheat oven to 375° F. Lightly spray a jelly-roll pan with cooking spray.

Arrange bread in a single layer on the prepared pan. Spray bread with cooking spray.

Bake for 7 to 10 minutes until crisp and lightly browned.

. . . . . . . . . . . . . . . . . . . . . . . . . . . . . . . . . . . . . .

**Recommended Wine:
Yogev Cabernet/Zinfandel Rosé**

Grilled salmon goes great with red wines while lettuce and salads generally call for white wine. The solution? Pick a rosé!

# { Hoisin-Glazed Chicken Thighs over Glass Noodles }

**Serves 4**

## Hoisin-Glazed Chicken Thighs over Glass Noodles

*Boneless chicken thighs are becoming commonplace at most butchers now, gaining popularity as a juicy alternative to white meat cutlets which tend to dry out if not cooked properly. Glass noodles are also called rice sticks. They are made from rice and are very easy to prepare.*

½ **cup hoisin sauce**

1 **(4-ounce) jar baby food plums**

1 **tablespoon minced garlic**

2 **tablespoons canola oil**

1 **pound boneless, skinless chicken thighs**

1 **pound glass noodles**

2 **quarts boiling water**

1 **½ cups fresh snow peas or 1 (9-ounce) package frozen, thawed**

1 **tablespoon sesame seeds**

2 **scallions, sliced diagonally**

In a small bowl, combine hoisin sauce with plums and garlic. Brush on chicken thighs.

Heat oil in a large sauté pan over medium heat. When oil is shimmering, place chicken in pan. Cook for 5 minutes on each side.

While chicken is cooking, prepare noodles: Place glass noodles in a large bowl. Pour boiling water over noodles and let sit for 8 minutes.

Add snow peas and sesame seeds to the pan with chicken. Cook for 2 minutes more.

Drain noodles and place in 4 bowls.

Remove chicken from the pan and slice it crosswise. Spoon snow peas with sauce over noodles. Distribute chicken among the bowls. Garnish with scallions.

## What is Hoisin Sauce?

*A dark, thick, sweet, and pungent Chinese condiment aka Chinese barbeque sauce, hoisin sauce is popular in Asian cooking, especially in stir-fries and marinades. It's a mixture of soy bean paste, garlic, vinegar, chilies, and sweetener. Hoisin sauce is characterized by its strong salty and slightly sweet flavor. For a gal who can't get enough of the sweet and salty flavor combo (chocolate covered pretzels are my fave!), hoisin sauce is right up my alley. A superb glaze for fish and meat, it's also a great secret ingredient for dipping sauce.*

**Recommended Wine:**
**Baron Herzog Old Vine Zinfandel**

These succulent chicken thighs, *pargiot* as they are referred to in Israel, are yet another example of a sweet and hearty dish that will pair well with a robust and jammy zinfandel.

# { Honey-Glazed Skewered Beef }
## Rice Pilaf with Fresh Tomatoes, Olives, and Parsley

**Serves 4** | While beef is marinating, begin rice pilaf.

## Honey-Glazed Skewered Beef

*If you use wooden skewers, they must be soaked in a shallow pan filled with enough water to cover them for an hour before you use them so they don't catch fire on the grill or under the broiler. After brushing the meat with the glaze, boil remaining glaze for 5 minutes to kill any bacteria from the raw meat. Before serving, brush the cooked glaze on the meat or serve on the side for dipping.*

- ½ **cup honey**
- ¼ **cup steak sauce**
- 2 **tablespoons Dijon mustard**
- 2 **tablespoons freshly squeezed orange juice**
- ¼ **teaspoon cinnamon**
- 2 **pounds cubed beef minute steak (10 to 12 pieces per pound, each about 1- x 1-inch)**

Heat grill to medium.

In a small bowl, mix together honey, steak sauce, mustard, orange juice, and cinnamon to make glaze.

Thread 5 to 6 cubes of beef on each skewer. Brush meat cubes with glaze.

Grill for 8 to 10 minutes for medium doneness (or grill to your desired doneness). Instead of grilling the beef cubes, you can broil them in your oven for about 6 to 8 minutes. Keep an eye on them to make sure they don't burn.

Place on serving platter and serve with Rice Pilaf with Fresh Tomatoes, Olives, and Parsley.

## Rice Pilaf with Fresh Tomatoes, Olives, and Parsley

- 2 **tablespoons olive oil**
- 1 **cup instant rice**
- ½ **cup angel hair, broken into 1- inch pieces**
- 1 **cup Manischewitz All Natural Vegetable Broth**
- 1 **medium tomato, chopped**
- ¼ **cup chopped pitted black olives, drained**
- ¼ **cup chopped fresh parsley**
  - **Kosher salt**
  - **Freshly ground black pepper**

Heat olive oil in a medium saucepan over medium heat. Stir in rice and pasta; mix well. Continue cooking, uncovered, over medium heat for 3 to 4 minutes, stirring occasionally.

Add vegetable broth; stir and cover. Remove from heat.

Let sit for 7 minutes. Stir in tomatoes, olives, parsley, salt and pepper to taste.

**Recommended Wine:**
**Herzog Reserve Cabernet/ Zinfandel/Syrah blend**

The beef is screaming for a big red cabernet sauvignon, while the sweet sauce can use the extra kick provided by zinfandel.

# { Knockwurst with Sauerkraut and Potatoes }

**Serves 8**

## Knockwurst with Sauerkraut and Potatoes

*Store-bought bags of shredded carrots can help you cut down your time at the grater.*

2   tablespoons canola oil

1   medium onion, coarsely chopped

2   (16-ounce) packages beef knockwurst

1   (32-ounce) jar sauerkraut, drained

1   cup shredded carrots

1   clove garlic, minced

1   tablespoon caraway seeds

2   cups Manischewitz All Natural Chicken Broth

6   medium potatoes, peeled and quartered

¼   cup chopped parsley

In a large heavy-bottomed saucepan, heat oil over medium heat. Add onions and knockwurst, cook for 5 minutes, turning often.

Add sauerkraut, carrots, garlic, caraway seeds, and broth; stir to combine. Nestle potatoes into knockwurst and sauerkraut. Cover and cook over high heat for 25 minutes or until potatoes are fork tender.

Sprinkle with parsley prior to serving.

## What's a Knockwurst?

*Knockwurst gets it name from the German words "knack" (crack) and "wurst" (sausage), because of the crackling sound made when the juices explode the first time it is cut into. Knockwurst are shorter, thicker, and more heavily seasoned than hot dogs and are traditionally served with sauerkraut.*

**Recommended Wine:**
**Alfasi Merlot**

This knockwurst and vegetable dish will marry nicely with a light-bodied red wine.

# { Lamb Meatballs in Pita }
## Cucumber, Tomato, and Avocado Relish

. . . . . . . . . . . . . . . . . . . . . . . . . . . . . . . . . . . . . . . . . . . . . . . . . . . . . . . . . . . . . . . . . . . . . .

**Serves 4** | Yield 24 meatballs. Make the salad while the meatballs are baking.

## Lamb Meatballs in Pita

**Gefen Canola Oil Cooking Spray**

4 **pitas with pockets**

1 **pound ground lamb**

¼ **cup finely chopped fresh mint**

1 **teaspoon ground cumin**

1 **teaspoon ground coriander**

½ **teaspoon turmeric**

¼ **teaspoon ground cinnamon**

¼ **teaspoon cayenne pepper**

1 **teaspoon kosher salt**

**Tahini for serving (optional)**

Preheat oven to 350° F. Line a jelly-roll pan with foil and spray the foil with cooking spray.

Combine lamb, mint, cumin, coriander, turmeric, cinnamon, cayenne, and salt in a medium bowl. Mix well. Form into 1-inch meatballs. Place on prepared pan and bake for 20 minutes. Remove from oven and let rest in the pan for 2 minutes.

While meatballs are baking, warm pitas in a dry skillet for 30 seconds on each side or in the oven for 3 to 5 minutes. Cover pitas in foil to keep warm.

To assemble: Slit one edge of pita to make a pocket. In each pita, layer two or three meatballs, a scoop of Cucumber, Tomato, and Avocado Relish, two or three meatballs, and another scoop of relish. Drizzle with tahini, if desired.

Serve extra Cucumber, Tomato, and Avocado Relish on the side.

## Cucumber, Tomato, and Avocado Relish

1 **English cucumber, peeled, and coarsely chopped**

2 **tomatoes, coarsely chopped**

1 **avocado, pitted, peeled, and coarsely chopped**

1 **clove garlic, minced**

2 **tablespoons freshly squeezed lemon juice**

1 **teaspoon kosher salt**

½ **teaspoon freshly ground black pepper**

1 **tablespoon torn fresh cilantro leaves**

In a medium bowl, place cucumbers, tomatoes, avocado, garlic, lemon juice, salt, pepper, and cilantro. Gently toss.

. . . . . . . . . . . . . . . . . . . . . . . . . . . . . . . . . . . . . . .

**Recommended Wine:**
**Ovadia Estates Barolo by Bartenura**

These well-seasoned meatballs, made from lamb, will pair wonderfully with a gamey red wine. Try an Old World wine such as an Italian Barolo.

# { Lebanese Herbed Lamb Chops with Pan Juices }
## Toasted Pine Nut Couscous

**Serves 4** | While lamb is cooking, prepare couscous.

## Lebanese Herbed Lamb Chops with Pan Juices

- 1   **tablespoon dried oregano**
- ½   **tablespoon garlic powder**
- 1   **teaspoon kosher salt**
- ½   **teaspoon ground allspice**
- ½   **teaspoon ground cinnamon**
- 4   **(6- to 8-ounce) shoulder lamb chops**
- 2   **tablespoons canola oil**
- 1   **shallot, minced**
- ½   **cup Manischewitz All Natural Beef Broth**

To make rub for chops: In a small bowl, combine oregano, garlic, salt, allspice, and cinnamon. Rub on both sides of chops.

In a large sauté pan, heat oil over medium heat. When oil is shimmering, place the chops in the pan. Cook for 4 minutes and turn; cook for another 4 minutes.

When chops are done, remove them from the pan and drain off fat. Add shallots; cook for 1 minute.

Add broth, stirring to incorporate all the browned bits from the pan. Continue cooking to reduce liquid by half, approximately 4 to 5 minutes.

Serve lamb chops over Toasted Pine Nut Couscous on a large serving platter; pour pan juices over the top.

## Toasted Pine Nut Couscous

- 1   **(7-ounce) box couscous**
- 1   **cup pine nuts**
- ½   **cup golden raisins**

Preheat oven to 350° F.

Spread pine nuts on a rimmed baking pan and bake for 6 minutes or until golden. Keep an eye on them so they do not burn. Let cool.

Prepare couscous according to package instructions. When couscous is done, stir in pine nuts and raisins. Mix lightly to combine.

**Recommended Wine:**
**Binyamina "Ruby" Syrah**

With its gamey, earthy, and herbaceous character, Syrah is a natural pairing for lamb chops.

# { Loaded Baked Potato }
## Chopped Salad

**Serves 6** | While potatoes are baking, prepare Chopped Salad.

## Loaded Baked Potato

6 (8-ounce) Idaho potatoes
1 tablespoon canola oil
1 medium onion, coarsely chopped
1 (1-pound) bag frozen broccoli florets, thawed
1 cup regular or low-fat sour cream
1 tablespoon kosher salt
1 teaspoon freshly ground black pepper
2 cups Les Petites Fermieres Shredded Cheddar

Preheat oven to 350° F.

Prick the potatoes with a fork and cook in the microwave on high for 12 minutes. While potatoes are in the microwave, heat oil in a large sauté pan over medium heat. Sauté onions in oil until translucent, about 5 minutes. Stir in broccoli.

When potatoes are done, cut them in half and scoop out the flesh. Mash the flesh with sour cream, salt, and pepper; and put the mixture back into the skins, filling them about three-quarters full. Distribute broccoli and onions evenly among the potato halves and top with cheese.

Bake for 15 minutes or until cheese is bubbly and the potatoes are heated through.

Serve with Chopped Salad.

## Chopped Salad

1 cucumber, sliced and quartered
1 small red onion, coarsely chopped
2 tomatoes, coarsely chopped
2 cups shredded iceberg lettuce, about ½ head
1 cup shredded carrots
1 ½ teaspoons Dijon mustard
1 ½ teaspoons honey
¼ teaspoon kosher salt
⅓ cup apple cider vinegar
⅔ cup canola oil
  Pinch freshly ground black pepper

In a large bowl, combine cucumber, onions, tomatoes, lettuce, and shredded carrots.

In a small bowl, whisk together mustard, honey, salt, vinegar, oil, and pepper to taste. Toss the salad with dressing to taste. Serve the remaining dressing on the side.

**Recommended Wine:
Bartenura Pinot Grigio**

With broccoli, onions, and cheddar cheese, this dish will work best with a crisp, palate-cleansing wine.

# { Herb Focaccia }
## Minestrone with Cheese Tortellini

**Serves 8** | Prepare Herb Focaccia first. While the focaccia is baking, make the minestrone.

## Herb Focaccia

**Gefen Canola Oil Cooking Spray**

¼ **cup olive oil**

½ **teaspoon dried basil**

½ **teaspoon dried oregano**

½ **teaspoon dried thyme**

2 **cloves garlic, minced**

1 **(12-ounce) container refrigerated pizza dough**

1 **teaspoon kosher salt**

Preheat oven to 425° F. Lightly spray an 11- x 13-inch jelly-roll pan with cooking spray.

Heat oil in a small saucepan over low heat. Add basil, oregano, and thyme; cook for 4 minutes. Remove from heat and stir in garlic. Set aside.

Spread dough on prepared pan, making a 10- x 12-inch rectangle. Make indentations with your fingertips all over dough. Pour the infused oil evenly over the dough.

Bake for 20 minutes, or until focaccia is deep golden brown. Sprinkle with salt and cut into squares to serve.

Serve with Minestrone with Cheese Tortellini.

## Minestrone with Cheese Tortellini

2 **tablespoons olive oil**

1 **medium onion, coarsely chopped**

1 **medium green pepper, seeds and ribs removed, coarsely chopped**

2 **cloves garlic, finely chopped**

2 **(32-ounce) boxes Manischewitz All Natural Vegetable Broth**

1 **(28-ounce) can chopped tomatoes, undrained**

1 **tablespoon kosher salt**

1 **teaspoon freshly ground black pepper**

1 **(16-ounce) bag California-style frozen mixed vegetables, not thawed**

1 **(15 ½-ounce) can kidney beans, rinsed and drained**

1 **(16-ounce) bag cheese tortellini**

½ **cup chopped fresh basil**

½ **cup Natural & Kosher Grated Parmesan**

Heat oil in large stockpot over medium heat. Add onions and peppers; cook for 5 to 7 minutes. Add garlic and cook for 30 seconds. Stir in broth, tomatoes, salt, pepper, frozen vegetables, and kidney beans. Bring to a boil and add tortellini. Cook for about 10 minutes or until tortellini float to the top. Ladle into bowls, garnish with basil and cheese, and serve with Herb Focaccia.

**Recommended Wine:**
**Binyamina Yogev Cabernet/Shiraz**

The herbs on the focaccia and the heartiness of the tomato-based minestrone will pair nicely with an herbaceous red wine.

# { Miso-Glazed Salmon with Jasmine Rice }
## Steamed Snow Peas and Carrots

**Serves 4** | While rice and salmon are cooking, prepare Steamed Snow Peas and Carrots.

## Miso-Glazed Salmon with Jasmine Rice

*Miso paste is a Japanese seasoning that is usually made with soybeans, rice, barley, and salt. It is high in protein and rich in vitamins and minerals. Jasmine rice has a nice sweet perfume that goes well with Miso-Glazed Salmon.*

**Gefen Canola Oil Cooking Spray**

1 **cup jasmine rice**

⅓ **cup packed dark brown sugar**

2 **tablespoons soy sauce**

¼ **cup miso paste**

¼ **cup hot water**

1 **teaspoon minced garlic**

4 **(6-ounce) salmon filets**

**Chopped fresh chives or scallions, for garnish**

Position oven rack so that it is 8 inches from the broiler. Preheat broiler to high. Lightly spray an 8- x 8-inch baking dish with cooking spray.

Prepare rice according to package instructions.

In a small bowl, prepare glaze: Whisk together brown sugar, soy sauce, miso, hot water, and garlic.

Place fish in a single layer in prepared dish. Drizzle glaze over salmon.

Broil fish for 15 minutes or until fish flakes easily with a fork.

Transfer salmon to a serving platter and garnish with chopped chives or scallions. Serve with Steamed Snow Peas and Carrots and jasmine rice.

## Steamed Snow Peas and Carrots

2 **cups snow peas, trimmed**

2 **cups packaged shredded carrots**

**Kosher salt**

**Freshly ground black pepper**

Place enough water in a saucepot to touch the bottom of the steamer basket. Place the pot over high heat. Steam snow peas and carrots together for about 5 minutes or until crisp-tender. Season with salt and pepper to taste.

**Recommended Wine:**
**Weinstock Cellar Select**
**Cabernet Sauvignon**

Salmon is a fatty fish with firm flesh. When glazed, it has enough flavor to hold up to a medium-bodied red wine.

# { Mushroom Pea Risotto }

## Greens and Vinaigrette

. . . . . . . . . . . . . . . . . . . . . . . . . . . . . . . . . . . . . . . . . . . . . . . . . . . . . . .

**Serves 6**

## Mushroom Pea Risotto

4   tablespoons olive oil, divided

2   cups sliced mixed fresh mushrooms

5   cups Manischewitz All Natural Vegetable Broth

1   tablespoon unsalted butter

⅓   cup finely minced onion or shallot

1   ½ cups Arborio rice

½   cup recommended white wine (see below)

¾   cup Natural & Kosher Grated Parmesan, plus more for serving

1   cup frozen peas, thawed

1   tablespoon chopped fresh parsley

In a sauté pan, heat 2 tablespoons olive oil and cook mushrooms over high heat for 5 minutes. Set aside.

In a medium saucepan, warm broth over medium-high heat. When broth comes to a simmer, reduce heat to very low and cover to keep warm.

While broth is warming, heat remaining 2 tablespoons olive oil and butter in a heavy 4-quart saucepan over medium heat. Add onions and cook, stirring, for 1 to 2 minutes, or until they begin to soften, being careful not to let them brown. Using a wooden spoon, stir rice into onions and mix well. Continue stirring for 1 minute, making sure all the grains are well coated. Add wine and stir until completely absorbed. Add ½ cup broth, stirring frequently until almost completely absorbed. Continue cooking rice, stirring in broth ½ cup at a time, allowing each addition to be almost completely absorbed before adding the next, until rice is tender but still firm, about 18 minutes total.

Turn off the heat; immediately add the cheese, mushrooms, peas, and parsley, mix well. Spoon risotto into a large serving bowl, top with additional cheese and serve immediately with Greens and Vinaigrette.

## Greens and Vinaigrette

2   tablespoons Bartenura Balsamic Vinegar

1   teaspoon Dijon mustard

¼   teaspoon kosher salt

3   tablespoons olive oil

1   (5-ounce) package salad greens, rinsed and dried

To make the vinaigrette: In a small bowl, whisk together vinegar, mustard, and salt. Slowly add oil. Place salad greens in a large serving bowl; toss with dressing and serve.

. . . . . . . . . . . . . . . . . . . . . . . . . . . . . . . . . . . . .

**Recommended Wine:**
**Pascal Bouchard Chablis (Chardonnay)**

The creamy risotto made with white wine, Parmesan, mushrooms, and peas is a sophisticated dish worthy of a fine white wine.

# { Niçoise Salad }

**Serves 4**

## Niçoise Salad

For salad:

- 1 **pound fresh string beans, rinsed, dried, and trimmed**
- 1 **pound small red-skinned potatoes, scrubbed and quartered**
- 1 **(1-pound) tuna steak**
- 1 **(8-ounce) jar quartered, marinated artichoke hearts, drained, marinade reserved**
- 8 **leaves romaine lettuce, rinsed and dried**
- 1 **red onion, halved lengthwise and thinly sliced**
- 1 **cup pitted oil-cured olives, drained**
- 2 **hard-cooked eggs, halved**
- 2 **on-the-vine tomatoes, cut in wedges**
- 1 **(15-ounce) can white beans, rinsed and drained**

For dressing:

- ¼ **cup white wine vinegar**
- 1 **tablespoon freshly squeezed lemon juice**
- 1 **clove garlic, crushed**
- 1 **teaspoon Dijon mustard**
- ½ **cup extra virgin olive oil**
- ½ **teaspoon kosher salt**
- ¼ **teaspoon freshly ground black pepper**

Fill a large bowl with cold water and ice cubes.

Steam string beans and potatoes for 12 to 15 minutes, until potatoes are fork tender. Drain vegetables and immediately plunge them into the ice water. Drain again.

While the vegetables are cooking, heat a large sauté pan over high heat.

Brush tuna with reserved marinade. Sear tuna 3 minutes on each side for medium-rare, or until desired doneness. Let cool slightly and cut into eight equal slices.

To assemble salad: Place 2 lettuce leaves on each of 4 plates. Distribute tuna, string beans, potatoes, artichoke hearts, onions, olives, eggs, tomatoes, and white beans among the plates.

To make dressing: In a small bowl, whisk together vinegar, lemon juice, garlic, and mustard. Slowly whisk in oil; season with salt and pepper.

Drizzle dressing over salad and serve with crusty bread.

Recommended Wine:
**Weinstock White by "W"**

Though tuna steaks have a firm enough flesh to hold up to red wine, when prepared as part of a salad like this Niçoise, a medium-bodied white wine makes a better pairing.

# { Oven-Baked Chicken Fingers with a Duo of Dipping Sauces }

## Garlic-Dusted French Fries

**Serves 8** | While chicken is baking, prepare Garlic-Dusted French Fries and honey mustard dipping sauce.

## Oven-Baked Chicken Fingers with a Duo of Dipping Sauces

*To save time, buy the chicken already cut in strips.*

**Gefen Canola Oil Cooking Spray**

4 **cups crushed cornflakes**

½ **cup matzoh meal**

1 **tablespoon kosher salt**

1 **teaspoon freshly ground black pepper**

½ **cup (¼-pound) pareve margarine, melted**

2 **pounds boneless, skinless chicken breasts, cut in ½-inch strips**

½ **cup Dijon mustard**

1 **cup honey**

1 **cup store-bought barbeque sauce**

Preheat oven to 425° F. Line a jelly-roll pan with foil and spray with cooking spray.

In a shallow bowl, combine cornflakes, matzoh meal, salt, and pepper. Place margarine in a second shallow bowl.

Dip each chicken strip in melted margarine. Roll strips in the cornflake mixture, pressing to coat. Transfer chicken to the prepared pan. Make sure you do not crowd the pan so chicken will bake up crisp. Bake for 20 minutes.

While chicken is baking, prepare honey mustard dipping sauce: Combine mustard with honey in a small bowl. Mix well.

Place chicken fingers on a serving platter. Serve with honey mustard and barbeque dipping sauces and Garlic-Dusted French Fries.

## Garlic-Dusted French Fries

1 **(32-ounce) bag frozen French fries**

1 **tablespoon kosher salt**

1 **teaspoon garlic powder**

Prepare fries according to package instructions.

In a small bowl, mix salt with garlic powder, and season fries before serving.

133

**Recommended Wine:**
**Binyamina Yogev**
**Cabernet Sauvignon/Merlot**

Chicken can go with either red or white wine; its pairing options largely depend on how it is prepared. Here, served with dipping sauces, a medium-bodied red will pair just fine.

# { Panko-Crusted Tilapia }
## Chili Mango Pasta

. . . . . . . . . . . . . . . . . . . . . . . . . . . . . . . . . . .

**Serves 4** | Prepare pasta first, then work on fish.

## Panko-Crusted Tilapia

- **4  (6-ounce) tilapia filets**
- **2  limes, divided**
- **Kosher salt**
- **Freshly ground black pepper**
- **½  cup unseasoned panko bread crumbs**
- **¼  cup matzoh meal**
- **¼  teaspoon chili powder**
- **2  large eggs**
- **2  tablespoons canola oil**

Rinse and dry tilapia. Squeeze juice from one lime over fish. Season with salt and pepper to taste.

In a shallow bowl or pie pan, mix panko with matzoh meal and chili powder.

In a second shallow bowl or pie pan, beat the eggs. Dip the fish in the beaten eggs and then in the panko mixture, coating evenly on both sides.

In a large skillet, heat oil over medium heat. Place breaded tilapia in pan. Brown on one side, about 3 minutes. Flip over and cook for 3 more minutes or until cooked through.

Remove fish from sauté pan and place on serving platter. Finish with an extra squeeze of lime juice.

Serve with lime wedges and Chili Mango Pasta.

## Chili Mango Pasta

*Be very careful when handling chili peppers. After touching the peppers, be sure to wash your hands before you touch any part of your face, especially your eyes. You can also use gloves or baggies to protect your hands. Seed and core a chili pepper as you would a regular pepper. The seeds and ribs contain most of the heat.*

- **1  pound angel hair or capellini**
- **1  mango, pitted, peeled, and cubed or 1 cup frozen mango cubes, thawed**
- **1  red chili pepper, seeds and ribs removed, finely minced**
- **1  medium red onion, coarsely chopped**
- **1  cup chopped fresh tomatoes**
- **2  tablespoons white wine vinegar**
- **½  teaspoon ground cinnamon**
- **1  teaspoon kosher salt**
- **½  teaspoon freshly ground black pepper**

Cook pasta according to package instructions.

While pasta is cooking, make sauce: In a large bowl, combine mango, chili pepper, onions, tomatoes, vinegar, cinnamon, salt, and pepper. Toss in hot pasta.

. . . . . . . . . . . . . . . . . . . . . . . . . . . . . . .

**Recommended Wine:**
**Goose Bay Sauvignon Blanc**

Tilapia is a flaky fish that can be easily over-powered by a heavy wine. Further, fried foods as well as sweet and spicy dishes such as the chili mango sauce, go great with crisp acidic white wines.

# { Pasta with Chicken and Olives }
## Heirloom Tomato Salad

. . . . . . . . . . . . . . . . . . . . . . . . . . . . . . . . . . . . . . . . . . . . . . .

**Serves 6** | Prepare tomato salad while chicken is marinating. Slice tomatoes and onions; dress just before serving

## Pasta with Chicken and Olives

*As a nice alternative, use whole pitted olives, serve the chicken unsliced and finish with extra rosemary.*

1   (1-pound) box fettuccine
6   boneless, skinless chicken cutlets, about 1 ½ pounds
    Freshly squeezed juice of 1 lemon
3   sprigs fresh rosemary or 1 ½ teaspoons dried
3   cloves garlic, minced
3   tablespoons olive oil
3   cups Manischewitz All Natural Chicken Broth
1   cup chopped oil-cured olives, drained
¼   cup chopped fresh flat leaf parsley
1   ½ teaspoons kosher salt

Cook pasta according to package instructions.

In a resealable plastic bag, place chicken, lemon juice, rosemary, and garlic; seal and let sit for 10 minutes.

In a large sauté pan, heat oil over medium heat. Remove chicken from the bag, add to the pan, and cook for 8 minutes on each side. Transfer chicken to a cutting board and cover it with foil to keep warm.

Add chicken broth to the pan, stirring to get the browned bits up. Add olives and cook for 10 minutes.

Slice chicken and place in a large serving bowl. Add cooked pasta, olives with broth, and parsley. Toss, season with salt, and serve with Heirloom Tomato Salad.

## Heirloom Tomato Salad

4   large heirloom tomatoes, sliced
1   red onion, halved lengthwise and sliced
1   teaspoon kosher salt
¼   teaspoon freshly ground black pepper
3   tablespoons olive oil
2   tablespoons Bartenura Balsamic Vinegar

Arrange tomatoes and onions decoratively on a plate. Season with salt and pepper. Drizzle olive oil and vinegar over the vegetables.

. . . . . . . . . . . . . . . . . . . . . . . . . . . . . . . . . . . .

**Recommended Wine:**
**Alfasi Reserve Malbec/Syrah**

Chicken breasts don't have the fat their dark meat counterparts have and often call for a lighter wine. But the robust flavors of garlic, rosemary, and balsamic vinegar can handle a heartier wine.

# { Polenta Stuffed with Mozzarella }
## Fennel and Celery Salad

. . . . . . . . . . . . . . . . . . . . . . . . . . . . . . . . . . . . . . . . . . . . . . . . . . . . . . . . . . . . . . . . . . .

**Serves 6** | Prepare Fennel and Celery Salad while polenta is in the oven.

## Polenta Stuffed with Mozzarella

**Gefen Canola Oil Cooking Spray**
1 **small onion, finely chopped**
2 **cups whole milk**
1 **(32-ounce) box Manischewitz All Natural Vegetable Broth**
2 **cups yellow cornmeal**
1 **teaspoon kosher salt**
2 **cups Natural & Kosher Shredded Mozzarella**
½ **cup Natural & Kosher Grated Parmesan**
2 **cups Gefen Classic Marinara Pasta Sauce**

Preheat oven to 350° F. Spray an 8-inch square baking pan with cooking spray.

Spray a small sauté pan with cooking spray. Over medium heat, cook onions until soft, about 5 minutes.

While the onions are cooking, heat milk with vegetable broth over medium heat in a large saucepan. Bring to a boil. Slowly whisk in cornmeal, making sure there are no lumps. Reduce heat to low and continue stirring until thickened. Add sautéed onions and salt.

Pour half of the polenta into the prepared baking pan. Sprinkle mozzarella and Parmesan overtop. Pour the rest of the polenta on top of the cheese. Bake for 25 minutes.

In the last 5 minutes of baking, warm tomato sauce in a medium saucepan over medium heat.

Scoop out portions of polenta onto dinner plates and top with tomato sauce. Serve with Fennel and Celery Salad.

## Fennel and Celery Salad

1 **fennel bulb, rinsed and dried**
4 **stalks celery, rinsed and dried**
1 **small red onion**
2 **tablespoons olive oil**
2 **tablespoons white wine vinegar**
2 **teaspoons coarsely chopped fresh thyme leaves**
1 **teaspoon orange zest**
1 **teaspoon kosher salt**
¼ **teaspoon freshly ground black pepper**

Remove the fronds from the fennel. Slice the fennel bulb in half lengthwise and peel off the discolored outer leaves.

Using a mandoline or a very sharp knife, slice fennel, celery, and onion into paper-thin slices and mix together in a large salad bowl.

In a small bowl, mix together olive oil, vinegar, thyme leaves, orange zest, salt, and pepper; and toss with the fennel, celery, and onion.

. . . . . . . . . . . . . . . . . . . . . . . . . . . . . . . . . . . .

**Recommended Wine:**
**Baron Herzog Merlot**

On its own, the polenta would do best with a creamy white wine. But with the red sauce, it becomes a great pairing for a medium-bodied red.

# { Ratatouille }
## Rice with Mozzarella and Basil

**Serves 6** | While the Ratatouille is cooking for the first 10 minutes, prepare the rice.

## Ratatouille

- **2 tablespoons olive oil**
- **1 medium onion, coarsely chopped**
- **1 green pepper, seeds and ribs removed, coarsely chopped**
- **1 eggplant, coarsely chopped**
- **1 zucchini, thinly sliced**
- **1 yellow squash, thinly sliced**
- **1 ½ tablespoons kosher salt**
- **1 teaspoon freshly ground black pepper**
- **1 (28-ounce) can diced tomatoes, undrained**
- **2 cloves garlic, minced**
- **½ cup chopped fresh basil**

Heat olive oil in a large saucepan over medium heat. Cook onions and peppers in oil for 5 minutes. Mix in eggplant, zucchini, and yellow squash. Season with salt and pepper. Mix well and continue cooking for 10 minutes, uncovered. Stir in tomatoes and garlic. Bring to boil; reduce heat to high simmer. Cook for 15 minutes.

Stir in basil and serve over Rice with Mozzarella and Basil.

## Rice with Mozzarella and Basil

- **4 cups Manischewitz All Natural Vegetable Broth**
- **1 teaspoon kosher salt**
- **2 cups long grain white rice**
- **1 cup Natural & Kosher Shredded Mozzarella**
- **½ cup Natural & Kosher Grated Parmesan**
- **2 tablespoons chopped fresh basil**

In a medium saucepan over high heat, bring vegetable broth and salt to a boil. Add rice, mix well, and cover. Reduce heat to simmer and cook for 20 minutes or until all broth has been absorbed. Remove from heat. Stir in cheeses and basil. Transfer to a serving bowl and top with Ratatouille.

**Recommended Wine:**
**Ovadia Estates Morellino Di Scansano**

The tomato base of this ratatouille makes it compatible with red wine. But a lighter red with sufficient acidity is needed here so as not to overpower the subtle flavors in the dish.

# { Salmon Burgers with Cucumber Dill Sauce }
## Sweet Iced Green Tea

............................................................

**Serves 6** | While burgers are cooking, make Cucumber Dill Sauce and Sweet Iced Green Tea.

## Salmon Burgers with Cucumber Dill Sauce

**Gefen Canola Oil Cooking Spray**

For burgers:

1   **(2-pound) salmon filet, skinned**
1   **large egg**
½   **cup plain bread crumbs**

For sauce:

1   **English cucumber, peeled, seeded, and finely chopped**
1   **clove garlic, finely minced**
¼   **cup finely chopped red onion**
1   **cup regular or low-fat plain yogurt**
½   **cup chopped fresh dill**
1 ½ **teaspoons kosher salt**
½   **teaspoon freshly ground black pepper**
6   **kaiser rolls**

Spray grill pan with cooking spray and place over high heat.

For burgers:
Cut salmon to fit in food processor bowl. Place salmon in the bowl of the food processor and pulse for 15 seconds, or finely chop by hand.

In a medium bowl, combine salmon with egg and bread crumbs. Form into 6 patties.

Place burgers on the pan, reduce heat to medium. Grill burgers for 6 minutes on each side, or until golden brown and done.

For sauce:
In a medium bowl, combine cucumber, garlic, onions, yogurt, dill, salt, and pepper.

Place each salmon burger in a kaiser roll with 2 tablespoons of Cucumber Dill Sauce.

Serve with Sweet Iced Green Tea.

## Sweet Iced Green Tea

*Simple syrup is the base for this refreshing drink. Green tea is loaded with antioxidants.*

For simple syrup:

½   **cup water**
½   **cup sugar**

For tea:

3   **bags green tea**
1   **quart boiling water**
1   **cup simple syrup**

For syrup:
In a small saucepan, combine water and sugar. Stir over medium heat until sugar dissolves.

For tea:
In a pot, steep tea bags in the water for 10 minutes. Remove tea bags. Stir in simple syrup. Chill tea in fridge or pour over ice and serve immediately.

............................................................

**Recommended Wine:**
**Red by W**

Salmon is a fatty fish that can handle a red wine. The dill sauce calls for a red that is medium-bodied with a balancing acidity.

# { Sausage Ragu with Penne }
## Tossed Antipasti

**Serves 6** | While sausage and penne are cooking, boil the eggs and prepare the Tossed Antipasti.

## Sausage Ragu with Penne

- 1   tablespoon olive oil
- 1   pound Italian-style beef sausage, casing removed, crumbled
- ¼   cup Bartenura Balsamic Vinegar
- 1   medium onion, coarsely chopped
- 1   medium green pepper, seeds and ribs removed, coarsely chopped
- 1   teaspoon dried oregano
- 1   (28-ounce) can crushed tomatoes, undrained
- 1   ½ teaspoons kosher salt
- 1   teaspoon crushed red pepper flakes
- 1   (1-pound) box penne

Heat olive oil in a medium saucepan over medium heat. Add crumbled sausage and cook for 5 minutes. Add vinegar, onions, and peppers; mix well. Cook for 10 minutes.

While sausage is cooking, prepare penne according to package instructions. Drain, place in a serving bowl, and set aside.

Stir oregano, tomatoes, salt, and red pepper flakes into the pan with sausage. Cook for 20 minutes more. Pour sauce over pasta; mix well. Serve with Tossed Antipasti.

## Tossed Antipasti

- ¼   pound salami, sliced into thin strips
- ½   cup sliced jarred roasted red peppers, drained
- ½   cup pitted black olives, drained
- ¼   cup jarred marinated artichoke hearts, drained
- 2   hard-cooked eggs, quartered
- 8   cups shredded romaine lettuce, rinsed and dried
- 3   teaspoons extra virgin olive oil
- 3   teaspoons red wine vinegar
- 1   teaspoon kosher salt
- ¼   teaspoon freshly ground black pepper

In a large salad bowl, combine salami, peppers, olives, artichoke hearts, eggs, and lettuce. Drizzle with olive oil and vinegar. Season with salt and pepper.

**Recommended Wine:**
**Ovadia Estates Barbera D'Alba**

Pasta with a sausage and tomato-based sauce? An Italian red is a sure bet!

# { Skillet Red Beans and Rice with Ground Beef }
## Corn Bread with Pepper Jelly

**Serves 6**

## Skillet Red Beans and Rice with Ground Beef

*Red Beans and Rice is a very popular New Orleans specialty. Now you can create an easy version using this recipe. Cajun seasoning mix usually includes salt with a variety of spices like garlic, onion, chilies, black pepper, mustard, and celery.*

2  tablespoons canola oil

1  pound ground beef

1  green pepper, seeds and ribs removed, coarsely chopped

1  medium onion, coarsely chopped

1  clove garlic, minced

1  (15 ½-ounce) can kidney beans, rinsed and drained

2  tablespoons Cajun seasoning

2  cups instant rice

2  cups Manischewitz All Natural Chicken Broth

¼  cup chopped scallions

Heat oil in a large sauté pan. Brown ground beef in oil, stirring to break up the meat, about 4 minutes. Add green pepper, onions, and garlic. Mix well and continue to cook until onions are transparent, 5 to 6 minutes. Add red beans and Cajun seasoning; mix well and cook for 2 minutes. Stir in rice and broth; cook for 5 minutes more.

Spoon into large bowls; garnish with scallions. Serve with Corn Bread with Pepper Jelly.

## Corn Bread with Pepper Jelly

1  jalapeño pepper, seeds and ribs removed, minced

½  cup finely chopped red pepper, seeds and ribs removed

1  tablespoon apple cider vinegar

1  (16-ounce) jar apple jelly

1  loaf store-bought corn bread

In a small saucepan, combine jalapeños, red peppers, vinegar, and jelly. Mix well and bring to boil. Reduce heat and simmer for 2 to 3 minutes.

Let cool about 5 minutes and serve with corn bread.

**Recommended Wine:**
**Flechas de Los Andes Gran Malbec**

The explosion of flavors in this dish from the beef, red beans, rice, and spices will bring to mind robust South American cuisine.

# { Sloppy Joes }
## Deviled Potato Salad

**Serves 4** | Boil potatoes and eggs while preparing Sloppy Joes, then assemble Deviled Potato Salad.

## Sloppy Joes

|   |   |
|---|---|
| 1½ | **tablespoons extra virgin olive oil** |
| ½ | **small onion, finely chopped** |
| ½ | **green pepper, seeds and ribs removed, finely chopped** |
| 1¼ | **pounds ground beef** |
| 2 | **tablespoons packed dark brown sugar** |
| 1 | **tablespoon McCormick Montreal Steak Seasoning** |
| ¼ | **cup Worcestershire sauce (see note page 245)** |
| 2 | **tablespoons tomato paste** |
| 4 | **crusty rolls, split in half, toasted** |

Heat olive oil in a 12-inch skillet over medium heat. Add onions and peppers, sauté until soft, about 5 minutes. Add beef to pan and cook until beef is browned, stirring frequently to break up the meat, about 5 minutes. Add brown sugar, steak seasoning, Worcestershire sauce, and tomato paste. Reduce heat to low and cook for 10 minutes, stirring occasionally.

Place rolls on a serving platter and distribute Sloppy Joe mixture evenly among the rolls. Serve with Deviled Potato Salad.

## Deviled Potato Salad

|   |   |
|---|---|
| 1 | **pound baby red-skinned potatoes, unpeeled, scrubbed, and halved** |
| 6 | **hard-cooked eggs, finely chopped** |
| 1 | **cup Israeli pickles, finely chopped** |
| 1 | **tablespoon kosher salt** |
| 1 | **teaspoon freshly ground black pepper** |
| ½ | **cup Gefen Regular or Lite Mayonnaise** |
| 1 | **tablespoon Dijon mustard** |
| 2 | **dashes Tabasco Sauce** |
| 1 | **teaspoon paprika, plus more for serving** |
| 1 | **tablespoon chopped fresh dill** |

Place potatoes in a pot with enough cold water to cover. Bring to boil and boil potatoes until fork tender, about 15 minutes. Rinse under cold water for 2 minutes to cool potatoes, drain well, and place in a large bowl.

Add eggs, pickles, salt, pepper, mayonnaise, mustard, Tabasco, paprika, and dill; toss to combine.

Sprinkle with additional paprika just before serving.

**Recommended Wine:**
**Alexander Reserve Cabernet Sauvignon**

This flavorful and hearty dish calls for a flavorful and hearty full-bodied wine. Try a rich cabernet sauvignon from Israel that is new to the market.

# { Smoked Turkey on Challah Rolls }
## Colorful Rice Salad

**Serves 6** | While the rice is cooking, prepare the salad ingredients and assemble the turkey sandwiches.

## Smoked Turkey on Challah Rolls

- 6 challah rolls, split in half
- 6 tablespoons Gefen Regular or Lite Mayonnaise
- 1 pound thinly sliced smoked turkey
- 6 slices on-the-vine tomatoes
- 6 leaves lettuce

Arrange challah rolls on a serving platter. Spread mayonnaise onto both halves of each roll. Distribute turkey, tomatoes, and lettuce on each roll. Serve with Colorful Rice Salad.

## Colorful Rice Salad

- Rice, any variety, to equal 3 cups cooked
- ½ red onion
- 1 red pepper, seeds and ribs removed
- 2 stalks celery
- 1 cup seedless red grapes
- 2 scallions, white and light green parts
- ½ cup frozen peas
- 1 tablespoon chopped fresh dill
- ¼ cup chopped fresh parsley
- Pine nuts (optional)
- 1 cup Basic Vinaigrette (see recipe page 43)

Prepare rice according to package instructions. Place in a serving bowl.

While rice is cooking, finely chop onion, pepper, and celery. Halve grapes. Thinly slice scallions. Rinse peas in cold water to thaw.

Combine onions, peppers, celery, grapes, scallions, peas, dill, parsley, and pine nuts with rice. Toss with vinaigrette to taste.

**Recommended Wine:**
**Clos de Nouys Vouvray (Chenin Blanc)**

This bright, low-fat meal screams for a nicely chilled white wine, maybe even one with a little sweetness to it.

# { Sole Amandine }
## Potatoes with Parsley Chive Butter

. . . . . . . . . . . . . . . . . . . . . . . . . . . . . . . . . . . . . . . . . . . . . . . . . . . .

**Serves 4** | Start by steaming the potatoes. While the potatoes are steaming, prepare Sole Amandine.

## Sole Amandine

*Butter has a low smoking point; take care that it doesn't burn. If it burns, discard it and start over.*

¼  **cup flour**

½  **teaspoon kosher salt**

¼  **teaspoon freshly ground black pepper**

4  **(6-ounce) sole filets**

3  **tablespoons butter, divided**

2  **tablespoons olive oil**

⅓  **cup slivered almonds**

   **Lemon wedges**

Preheat oven to 250° F. Place a serving platter in the oven for a few minutes to warm. Turn off the oven.

Combine flour, salt, and pepper in a shallow bowl. Coat the fish with the flour mixture, shaking off any excess.

In a large sauté pan over medium-high heat, melt 2 tablespoons butter with oil. Place fish in the pan and cook for about 5 minutes. Gently turn fish and continue cooking for 3 minutes more. Transfer cooked fish to the warmed platter, leaving butter sauce in the pan. Add remaining 1 tablespoon butter.

Cook almonds in the pan for about 2 minutes, until just golden. Spoon almonds and butter sauce on top of fish.

Serve with lemon wedges and Potatoes with Parsley Chive Butter.

## Potatoes with Parsley Chive Butter

1  **pound baby red-skinned potatoes, unpeeled, scrubbed and halved**

4  **tablespoons butter, at room temperature**

2  **tablespoons chopped fresh flat leaf parsley**

2  **tablespoons chopped fresh chives**

1  **teaspoon kosher salt**

½  **teaspoon freshly ground black pepper**

Steam potatoes in vegetable steamer for 20 minutes or until fork tender. Remove potatoes from steamer and place in a medium mixing bowl. Add butter and toss until butter melts. Add parsley, chives, salt, and pepper. Mix thoroughly and serve.

. . . . . . . . . . . . . . . . . . . . . . . . . . . . . . . . . . . . . .

**Recommended Wine:**
**Herzog Reserve
Russian River Chardonnay**

These elegant sole filets, prepared and served with butter, call for a creamy white wine such as a rich chardonnay made in the style of a fine white Burgundy.

# { Spaghetti with Tomato and Basil }
## Green Beans with Shaved Parmesan

**Serves 6** | While tomato sauce is cooking, prepare green beans.

## Spaghetti with Tomato and Basil

*"Chiffonade" is a French term which means "rags." To make a chiffonade of basil: Stack the leaves and roll them into a tight cigar shape. Slice crosswise into thin strips. Fluff the strips to separate them.*

1   (1-pound) box thin spaghetti
6   tablespoons extra virgin olive oil
1   red onion, halved lengthwise and thinly sliced
1   (28-ounce) can diced tomatoes, undrained
3   tablespoons red wine vinegar
2   teaspoons Gefen Coarse Sea Salt
1   teaspoon freshly ground black pepper
1   bunch basil, rinsed, patted dry, in a chiffonade
    Store-bought crusty Italian bread

Cook spaghetti according to package instructions.

While spaghetti is cooking, prepare sauce: In a 4-quart saucepot over medium heat, heat oil and onions. Cook until soft, about 5 minutes. Add tomatoes and vinegar; cook for 15 minutes. Season with salt and pepper.

Drain spaghetti and add to tomato mixture. Toss well.

Toss in basil just before serving. Serve immediately with Green Beans with Shaved Parmesan and warmed bread.

## Green Beans with Shaved Parmesan

3   tablespoons olive oil
1   clove garlic, minced
1   pound fresh green beans, trimmed, rinsed, and drained
1   teaspoon Gefen Coarse Sea Salt
½   teaspoon freshly ground black pepper
1   tablespoon freshly squeezed lemon juice
¼   cup shaved Natural & Kosher Parmesan

In a medium sauté pan over low heat, heat oil and add garlic. Cook for 2 minutes. Add beans, salt, pepper, and lemon juice. Stir and cover. Cook for 5 minutes. Place in serving bowl and top with shaved Parmesan.

**Recommended Wine:**
**Ovadia Estates Chianti**

This flavorful classic Italian dish will go great with a classic Italian red wine.

# { Spaghettini with Tuna }

**Serves 6**

## Spaghettini with Tuna

*Use a good quality tuna. The better the tuna, the better this dish will be.*

1    (1-pound) box spaghettini (thin spaghetti)
¼    cup olive oil
2    cloves garlic, minced
2    (6-ounce) cans tuna in oil, undrained
2    cups Manischewitz All Natural Vegetable Broth
3    tablespoons finely chopped fresh parsley

Prepare pasta according to package instructions.

In a medium saucepan, heat oil over low heat. Add garlic and cook for 2 minutes, until fragrant, being careful not to burn. (If it burns, garlic will taste bitter. Throw it out and start over.) Add tuna with the oil from the can; mix well. Stir in broth, increase heat to medium. Cook for 10 minutes, stirring occasionally, being careful not to break up the tuna too much. Add parsley and cook for 1 to 2 minutes more, stirring occasionally. Pour over spaghettini and serve with crusty bread.

## Perfect for Tuna Fans

*This dish is based on the Italian Spaghetti al Tonno. It is a perfect meal for anyone who doesn't eat meat or poultry but does eat fish—or for that tough cookie in your house who won't try any "seafood" except gefilte fish or canned tuna. (I'm not naming any names but if you've read my books you know who I mean.) You can spice up this dish, literally, by adding red pepper flakes and a 28-ounce can of whole plum tomatoes. (Break them up with your spoon while stirring and cooking.) This easy dish is an Italian staple—why not a kosher one too?*

**Recommended Wine:**
**Goose Bay Sauvignon Blanc**

Fish can often taste metallic with red wines. Here is a good opportunity to go for a bottle of your favorite white wine.

# { Spice-Rubbed Grilled Chicken }

## Fruit Salsa

**Serves 4** | Prepare salsa while chicken is grilling.

## Spice-Rubbed Grilled Chicken

*The mixture of spices and salt are called a rub because that's what you do with it—rub it onto the meat.*

| | |
|---|---|
| 1 | tablespoon onion powder |
| 1 | tablespoon kosher salt |
| 1 | tablespoon dried thyme leaves |
| 1 | teaspoon ground allspice |
| ½ | teaspoon ground cinnamon |
| ½ | teaspoon cayenne pepper |
| 8 | chicken legs with thighs, with skin |
| ¼ | cup canola oil |

Heat grill or grill pan to medium-high heat.

In a small bowl, whisk together onion powder, salt, thyme, allspice, cinnamon, and cayenne pepper.

In a large bowl, coat chicken with oil. Rub spices onto each piece of chicken.

Grill chicken, 12 minutes on each side, or until juices run clear when the chicken is pierced with a fork.

Transfer chicken to a serving platter, top with Fruit Salsa and serve with store-bought potato salad.

## Fruit Salsa

*This is a refreshing summer dish when watermelon and blueberries are at their best. Fun for outdoor or indoor grilling!*

| | |
|---|---|
| 1 | cup coarsely chopped fresh mango |
| ½ | cup fresh blueberries, rinsed and dried |
| 1 | cup coarsely chopped, seeded watermelon |
| 1 | medium red onion, coarsely chopped |
| 1 | jalapeño, seeded and finely chopped |
| 1 | medium tomato, coarsely chopped |
| ¼ | cup finely chopped fresh cilantro |
| 1 | tablespoon kosher salt |
| | Freshly squeezed juice of 1 lime |

Combine mangoes, blueberries, watermelon, onions, jalapeños, tomatoes, cilantro, salt, and lime juice together in a large bowl. Serve over grilled chicken.

**Recommended Wine:**
**Carmel Appellation Carignan**

Chicken legs and thighs are richer than breasts and, especially when grilled with a flavorful rub, can easily handle red wines.

# { Spicy Spinach Miso Soup with Udon Noodles }
## Wonton Crisps

. . . . . . . . . . . . . . . . . . . . . . . . . . . . . . . . . . . . . . . . . . . . . . .

**Serves 4** | Prepare Wonton Crisps first. While they are baking, make soup.

## Spicy Spinach Miso Soup with Udon Noodles

1   (9-ounce) package Japanese udon-style noodles

8   tablespoons miso paste

1   bunch baby spinach, rinsed, dried, and coarsely chopped

1   tablespoon red chili flakes

2   scallions, white part and 3 to 4 inches of light green, sliced diagonally

¼   cup fresh cilantro leaves

Prepare noodles according to package instructions.

In a medium pot over high heat, bring 4 cups water to a boil. Reduce heat to medium. Whisk miso paste into water until paste is dissolved.

Divide spinach and chili flakes evenly among 4 soup bowls. Ladle miso broth and noodles into bowls. Top each bowl with scallions and cilantro. Serve with Wonton Crisps.

## Wonton Crisps

**Gefen Canola Oil Cooking Spray**

24  wonton wrappers

1   ½ teaspoons sesame oil

1   ½ tablespoons canola oil

1   ½ tablespoons black sesame seeds

1   ½ tablespoons white sesame seeds

Preheat oven to 350° F. Line two jelly-roll pans with foil and spray with cooking spray.

In a small bowl, mix together sesame and canola oils.

Arrange wonton wrappers on prepared pans. Brush each wrapper with oils.

Sprinkle sesame seeds on top. Bake for about 8 minutes or until golden.

. . . . . . . . . . . . . . . . . . . . . . . . . . . . . . . . . . .

**Recommended Wine:**
**Herzog Selection Blanc de Blancs Brut**

Pairing soup with wine is difficult as the texture of two liquids makes it difficult to complement one with the other. The best solution for this… try a sparkling wine.

# { Stacked Eggplant Rounds }
## Braised Carrots

**Serves 4** | While eggplants are cooking, after you've made the feta mixture and cut the basil, prepare the Braised Carrots.

## Stacked Eggplant Rounds

*To seed tomatoes, cut tomato in half and gently scoop out seeds; or turn halves upside down over a bowl and gently squeeze until all the seeds have come out. Tomato seeds can be bitter and so can eggplant; so it is better to remove the seeds for this recipe.*

**Gefen Canola Oil Cooking Spray**
2 **eggplants, unpeeled, sliced into ½-inch rounds**
**Kosher salt**
¼ **cup olive oil**
¼ **teaspoon freshly ground black pepper**
1 **(8-ounce) container feta cheese, crumbled**
6 **on-the-vine tomatoes, seeded and chopped or
1 (16-ounce) can chopped tomatoes, drained**
1 **green pepper, seeds and ribs removed, finely chopped**
8 **large basil leaves**

Preheat oven to 425° F. Lightly spray jelly-roll pan with cooking spray.

Place eggplant slices on paper towels and sprinkle lightly with salt. Let sit for about 5 minutes. Pat dry with more paper towels.

Lay the eggplant rounds in a single layer on prepared pan. Brush with olive oil and season with pepper. Roast for 15 minutes; turn over and brush with oil. Continue roasting for 10 minutes more.

While eggplant is roasting, combine feta, tomatoes, and peppers in a medium bowl. Set aside.

Stack basil leaves, roll them up like a cigar, and slice them into thin strips (a chiffonade).

Place one slice eggplant on a serving platter. Spoon 1 to 2 tablespoons feta mixture on top. Repeat layers. Finish with a few shreds basil. Repeat with remaining ingredients.

Serve with Braised Carrots.

## Braised Carrots

1 **(16-ounce) bag peeled baby carrots**
3 **tablespoons butter**
2 **cloves garlic, smashed**
1 **tablespoon kosher salt**
3 **tablespoons minced fresh parsley**

In a medium saucepan over high heat, place carrots, butter, garlic, and salt. Cover with water and cook, uncovered, for 8 to 10 minutes, or until carrots are cooked. Drain carrots, remove garlic clove, and stir in parsley.

. . . . . . . . . . . . . . . . . . . . . . . . . . . . . . . . .
Recommended Wine:
**Carmel Private Collection Chardonnay**

Though eggplant brings to mind red sauce, this dish is made with herbs and cheese. Chill your favorite chardonnay and serve.

# { Steak with Pan Sauce }
## Pommes Frites

**Serves 2** | Prepare Pommes Frites first and then cook steaks.

## Steak with Pan Sauce

*This type of preparation is called "à la minute," meaning right away when you order it.*

- 2  (8-ounce) bone-in or 2 (6-ounce) boneless rib-eye steaks
- 2  teaspoons kosher salt
- 1  teaspoon cracked black pepper
- 4  tablespoons canola oil
- 2  medium shallots, minced
- 4  tablespoons recommended red wine (see below)
- ½  cup Manischewitz All Natural Beef Broth

Season steaks with salt and pepper.

In a large sauté pan, heat oil over high heat. Place steaks in the pan and sear for 1 minute. Reduce heat to medium-high and cook for 3 minutes on each side for medium doneness. Transfer steaks to 2 dinner plates and cover with foil to keep warm.

Add shallots and red wine to the pan; cook for 1 minute. Stir in broth and continue cooking for about 4 minutes, or until sauce is reduced by half.

Pour sauce over steaks and serve with Pommes Frites.

## Pommes Frites

*Pommes frites means fried potatoes in French. This process of frying the potatoes twice is called blanching. It helps the potato get a crunchy skin.*

- 2  Idaho potatoes
- 4  cups canola oil
- 2  teaspoons kosher salt
- ½  teaspoon cracked black pepper

Peel potatoes and cut into ⅓-inch thick strips. As you cut, place potatoes into a large bowl filled with cold water.

In a large heavy-bottomed pan over medium heat, heat oil to 325° F.

While oil is heating, drain potatoes and dry well.

Cover a work surface with a layer of paper towels.

Place potatoes in oil and cook for 5 minutes. Remove with a slotted spoon and place on the paper towels to drain and cool, about 2 minutes.

Increase the heat of the oil to 375° F. Place the potatoes back into the oil for 2 to 3 minutes or until golden. Remove with slotted spoon and drain on paper towels. Season with salt and pepper.

**Recommended Wine:**
**Herzog Reserve**
**Chalk Hill Cabernet Sauvignon**

There are few natural pairings better than steak and red wine. Grab a robust red such as a cabernet sauvignon and savor the deliciousness!

# { Stuffed Peppers }
## Cucumber and Red Onion Salad

. . . . . . . . . . . . . . . . . . . . . . . . . . . . . . . . . . . . . . . . . . . . . . . . . . . . . . . .

**Serves 4** | While peppers are baking, prepare Cucumber and Red Onion Salad.

## Stuffed Peppers

4  **large peppers**

4  **cups boiling water**

1  **tablespoon canola oil**

1  **pound ground beef**

1  **medium onion, coarsely chopped**

1  **tablespoon kosher salt**

1  **teaspoon freshly ground black pepper**

2  **cups cooked instant rice**

¼  **cup chopped fresh dill**

   **Pinch ground nutmeg**

1  **(28-ounce) can chopped tomatoes, undrained**

Preheat oven to 350° F.

To prepare peppers: Cut off tops of peppers. Reach in with your fingers or a large spoon and gently remove the seeds and ribs, making sure to leave peppers whole so they can be stuffed. Set aside the pepper tops. Place the whole peppers in a 9-inch square baking pan and pour boiling water in them. Set aside.

Finely chop pepper tops.

In a medium sauté pan, heat oil over medium-high heat. Crumble the ground beef into the pan. Mix in the onions and pepper tops. Season with salt and pepper. Mix well and cook for 5 minutes. Stir in cooked rice, dill, and nutmeg; mix well.

Drain peppers and stuff them with beef mixture. Return peppers to the baking pan. Pour tomatoes over and around peppers and bake for 20 minutes.

Arrange peppers and tomatoes on a serving platter and serve with Cucumber and Red Onion Salad.

## Cucumber and Red Onion Salad

1  **cucumber, unpeeled, rinsed, and sliced**

1  **red onion, halved lengthwise and thinly sliced**

¼  **cup Basic Vinaigrette (see recipe page 43)**

In a salad bowl, mix cucumber and red onion with ¼ cup Basic Vinaigrette. Toss and serve.

. . . . . . . . . . . . . . . . . . . . . . . . . . . . . . . . . . . . . . . .

**Recommended Wine:**
**Herzog Reserve**
**Napa Valley Cabernet Sauvignon**

This hearty dish with ground beef makes for the perfect robust red wine pairing.

# { Sweet and Spicy Turkey Burgers }
## Sweet Potato Wedges

. . . . . . . . . . . . . . . . . . . . . . . . . . . . . . . . . . . . . . . . . . . . . . . . . . . . . . . . . .

**Serves 6** | Make potatoes first. While potatoes are baking, prepare Sweet and Spicy Turkey Burgers.

## Sweet and Spicy Turkey Burgers

*Although this mixture is very wet when you form the patties, the juices get absorbed while the burgers cook.*

| 1 | ½ pounds ground turkey
| 1 | cup store-bought barbeque sauce, plus more for serving
| 1 | cup plain bread crumbs
| ½ | cup packed dark brown sugar
| 1 | large egg, beaten
| 1 | tablespoon kosher salt
| 1 | teaspoon cracked black pepper
| | **Gefen Canola Oil Cooking Spray**
| 6 | whole wheat buns, split in half
| | Lettuce
| | Tomato
| | **Gefen Regular or Lite Mayonnaise**

In a large bowl, combine ground turkey, barbeque sauce, bread crumbs, brown sugar, egg, salt, and pepper. Form into 6 patties; place on a plate and chill in the fridge for 10 minutes.

Lightly spray a grill pan with cooking spray and heat pan over medium heat. Grill burgers about 7 minutes on each side or until cooked through.

Serve on whole wheat buns with lettuce, tomato, mayonnaise, barbeque sauce, and Sweet Potato Wedges.

## Sweet Potato Wedges

| | **Gefen Canola Oil Cooking Spray**
| 4 | large sweet potatoes
| 1 | tablespoon kosher salt
| 2 | teaspoons freshly ground black pepper
| | Canola oil

Preheat oven to 400° F. Line two jelly-roll pans with foil. Spray with cooking spray.

Peel potatoes and halve lengthwise. Cut each half into 4 wedges and place in a large bowl. Toss with oil, salt, and pepper. Place on prepared pans. Bake for 15 minutes. Remove from oven and turn the potatoes. Return to the oven and continue baking for another 15 minutes.

. . . . . . . . . . . . . . . . . . . . . . . . . . . . . . . . . . . . . . . . . . .

**Recommended Wine:**
**Weinstock Cellar Select Lodi Zinfandel**

Burgers—good ol' American fare—are worthy of an American wine. Grab a California zinfandel and enjoy.

# { Tex-Mex Mac and Cheese }
## Lemon Butter Broccoli

**Serves 6** | While macaroni and cheese is in the oven, prepare Lemon Butter Broccoli.

## Tex-Mex Mac and Cheese

*Try wagon wheels or other fun pasta shapes for the kids.*

  **Gefen Canola Oil Cooking Spray**
1 **(1-pound) box pasta shells**
2 **cups Les Petites Fermieres Shredded Cheddar**
2 **cups shredded Monterey Jack cheese**
1 **tablespoon kosher salt**
1 **teaspoon freshly ground black pepper**
1 **(16-ounce) can diced tomatoes, undrained**
½ **cup heavy cream**
1 **cup Natural & Kosher Grated Parmesan**

Preheat oven to 375° F. Spray a 7- x 10-inch baking dish with cooking spray.

Cook pasta according to package instructions.

In a large bowl, toss pasta with cheeses, salt, pepper, and tomatoes. Spoon into prepared dish.

Pour the cream over the pasta mixture. Adjust seasoning, if necessary. Top with Parmesan. Bake for 25 minutes and serve directly from the baking dish with Lemon Butter Broccoli on the side.

## Lemon Butter Broccoli

1 **(2-pound) bag frozen broccoli florets**
3 **tablespoons butter, softened**
1 **tablespoon kosher salt**
1 **½ tablespoons freshly squeezed lemon juice**

Prepare broccoli according to package instructions. When broccoli is crisp-tender, transfer to a bowl and toss with butter, salt, and lemon juice.

171

**Recommended Wine:**
**Barkan Classic Merlot**

Traditional macaroni and cheese might warrant a white wine. The addition of the tomatoes imparts flavors that will hold up to a medium-bodied red wine.

# { Thai Chicken Soup }
## Summer Rolls

**Serves 6** | While soup is simmering, prepare Summer Rolls.

## Thai Chicken Soup

*Lemongrass is a long, thick stalk of grass. Trim the end and bruise the stalk by crushing it with the back of a heavy knife or a wooden pestle.*

- 1 tablespoon canola oil
- 1 pound boneless, skinless chicken breast, cut into ¼-inch strips
- 1 (8-ounce) carton button mushrooms, wiped clean with paper towels, and quartered
- 5 cups Manischewitz Reduced Sodium All Natural Chicken Broth
- 2 tablespoons soy sauce
- Freshly squeezed juice of 1 lime
- 1 (14-ounce) can coconut milk
- 1 stalk lemongrass, bruised
- 1 jalapeño or Thai chili pepper, halved and seeded
- ¼ cup fresh cilantro leaves

Heat oil in a wok or large sauté pan over high heat. Add chicken and mushrooms, cook for about 5 minutes, stirring occasionally. Mix in broth, soy sauce, lime juice, coconut milk, lemongrass, and jalapeño. Bring to a boil; reduce heat and simmer, uncovered, for 10 minutes.

Remove and discard lemongrass, and jalapeño before serving.

Ladle soup into bowls and garnish with cilantro leaves. Serve with Summer Rolls.

## Summer Rolls

- ½ pound rice sticks
- 1 red pepper, seeds and ribs removed
- 1 English cucumber, peeled
- 2 scallions, white and light green parts
- 1 cup packaged shredded carrots
- 1 tablespoon sesame oil
- 12 rice paper wrappers
- ¼ cup whole fresh mint leaves
- 2 ½ tablespoons freshly squeezed lime juice
- 2 tablespoons store-bought chili sauce
- 2 tablespoons packed light brown sugar
- ⅓ cup store-bought Thai peanut sauce

Soak rice sticks in hot water for about 8 minutes, drain and set aside.

While rice sticks are soaking, prepare filling: Using a mandoline or sharp knife, thinly slice pepper, cucumber, and scallions. Place in a large bowl and mix in carrots, rice sticks, and sesame oil.

Fill a large shallow bowl with very warm water and slide one wrapper through the water, immersing for 5 seconds, to make wrapper pliable. Lay the wrapper flat on a work surface. Place a small amount of the rice stick and vegetable mixture along the bottom third of the wrapper. Be careful not to overstuff or the wrapper will tear. Top with a few mint leaves. Gently fold up the bottom of the wrapper to cover the filling. Fold in the right and left sides; and roll up like a tight cigar. Place on a serving platter and cover with a damp towel. Repeat with remaining wrappers and filling.

In a small bowl, mix lime juice, chili sauce, and brown sugar to make a dipping sauce. Spoon peanut sauce into a second small bowl.

Serve Summer Rolls with the two dipping sauces.

**Recommended Wine:
Ness Blanco by Elvi Wines**

The medley of herbs, spices, coconut milk, chicken breasts, and veggies requires a light-bodied wine with a palate-cleansing acidity.

# { Turkey Breast with Port Wine Cherry Sauce }
## Roasted Potatoes

. . . . . . . . . . . . . . . . . . . . . . . . . . . . . . . . . . . . . . . . . . . . . . . . . . . . . . . . . . . . . . . .

**Serves 4** | Make the potatoes first. While they are roasting, prepare the turkey breast.

## Turkey Breast with Port Wine Cherry Sauce

- 4  boneless, skinless turkey breast cutlets, about 2 pounds
- 1  teaspoon kosher salt
- ¼  teaspoon cracked black pepper
- 1  tablespoon canola oil
- 1  shallot, minced
- ½  cup Kedem Port Wine
- ½  cup Manischewitz All Natural Chicken Broth
- ½  cup canned or frozen pitted dark sweet cherries
- 1  sprig fresh rosemary leaves or ½ teaspoon dried

Season turkey with salt and pepper. Heat oil in a sauté pan over medium heat. Add turkey cutlets and cook for 3 to 4 minutes on each side or until thoroughly cooked. Transfer to a serving platter and cover with foil while preparing the sauce.

Add the shallots to the sauté pan and cook for about 1 minute. Add wine, broth, cherries, and rosemary. Cook until sauce is reduced by half, about 6 minutes.

Pour sauce over the cutlets and serve with Roasted Potatoes.

## Roasted Potatoes

- 1  pound fingerling potatoes, unpeeled and scrubbed
- 2  tablespoons canola oil
- 1  tablespoon kosher salt
- ½  teaspoon cracked black pepper

Preheat oven to 450° F.

Place potatoes in a 9- x 13-inch pan. Toss with oil, salt, and pepper to coat. Roast for 25 minutes, shaking the pan every once in a while.

. . . . . . . . . . . . . . . . . . . . . . . . . . . . . . . . . . . . . . . . . . . . . . .

**Recommended Wine:**
**Covenant Red C Cabernet Sauvignon**

Turkey breasts are lean, but the red port wine sauce and cherries make this a nice pairing for a red wine.

# { Vegetable Lo Mein }
## Frothy Jasmine Iced Tea

**Serves 6**

## Vegetable Lo Mein

*This Lo Mein recipe is full of robust flavors and healthful vegetables. Make sure you have all of your ingredients sliced, measured, and ready to go because each step takes only minutes. Use your time wisely: While the pasta is cooking, prepare vegetables.*

- 1 (1-pound) box thin linguine
- 1 head bok choy
- 1 cup fresh bean sprouts
- 1 bunch scallions
- 1 tablespoon canola oil
- 1 (1-pound) package frozen stir-fry vegetables, thawed and drained
- ½ cup ginger teriyaki sauce

Cook pasta according to package instructions.

While pasta is cooking, rinse and dry bok choy, bean sprouts, and scallions. Quarter bok choy lengthwise and thinly slice scallions.

Drain pasta and set aside.

In a large sauté pan or wok, heat oil over high heat. When the pan is very hot, add thawed vegetables and bok choy. Stir to combine and continue to cook and stir for 2 to 3 minutes.

Add cooked pasta and toss vegetables, stirring continually another 2 to 3 minutes. Add teriyaki sauce. Toss and continue cooking for another 1 to 2 minutes.

Remove from heat. Add sprouts and scallions and toss again.

Serve immediately with Frothy Jasmine Iced Tea.

## Frothy Jasmine Iced Tea

*My inspiration for this drink came from bubble tea which has been all the rage. So here is bubble tea without the bubbles. If you can't find jasmine tea, use Ceylon or Darjeeling.*

- 1 quart hot water
- ¼ cup superfine sugar
- 3 jasmine tea bags
- 2 cups soy milk
- 2 tablespoons freshly squeezed lemon juice
- 6 ice cubes, plus additional for serving

In a large pot, heat water until it just begins to boil. Stir in the sugar until it dissolves. Remove from heat. Place tea bags into water and let steep for about 3 minutes. Remove the tea bags.

In a blender, combine tea, soy milk, lemon juice, and ice. Blend until frothy, about 1 minute.

Serve over ice in tall glasses.

## Homemade Stir-Fry Sauce

*If you have more time, try this easy recipe and make your own stir-fry sauce: In a small bowl, mix together ⅔ cup hoisin sauce, ⅓ cup soy sauce, 1 tablespoon grated fresh ginger or 1 cube frozen crushed ginger and 1 tablespoon minced garlic or 1 cube frozen Gefen Crushed Garlic.*

**Recommended Wine:**
**Shiloh Cabernet Sauvignon/Merlot blend**

The robust flavors introduced by the ginger teriyaki sauce require a wine with both body and a fruity acidity.

# { Vegetarian Pad Thai }
## Thai Cucumber Salad

. . . . . . . . . . . . . . . . . . . . . . . . . . . . . . . . . . . . . . . . . . . . . . . . . . . . . . . . . . . . . . . . . . . . . . . . . . . . . .

**Serves 4** | Pad Thai should be served warm, so prepare the Thai Cucumber Salad first.

## Vegetarian Pad Thai

- 1 **(16-ounce) package rice stick noodles**
  **Boiling water**
- 1 **tablespoon finely chopped dried apricots**
- 1 **tablespoon finely chopped dates**
- 1 **tablespoon freshly squeezed lemon or lime juice**
- 1 **tablespoon smooth peanut butter**
- 2 **tablespoons packed dark brown sugar**
- 1 **tablespoon soy sauce**
- 1 **teaspoon chili sauce**
- ½ **cup Manischewitz All Natural Vegetable Broth**
- 2 **tablespoons canola oil**
- 3 **cloves garlic, minced**
- ½ **teaspoon grated fresh ginger**
- 1 **(14-ounce) container firm tofu**
- 1 **cup fresh bean sprouts, rinsed and dried**
- 1 **cup packaged shredded carrots**
- 2 **tablespoons snipped fresh chives**
- ¼ **cup torn fresh cilantro leaves**

Place rice noodles in a large bowl. Cover with boiling water and let sit for 8 minutes; drain.

Drain tofu on paper towels for 5 minutes and cut into ¾-inch cubes.

In a food processor, pulse apricots, dates, and lemon juice to make a paste. In a medium bowl, whisk together apricot paste, peanut butter, brown sugar, soy sauce, and chili sauce. While whisking, add up to ½ cup vegetable broth to form a thick but pourable sauce. Set aside.

Heat oil in a large sauté pan or wok, over very high heat. Add garlic, ginger, and tofu; toss gently and cook until tofu is browned, about 5 minutes. Turn off heat. Toss in bean sprouts, carrots, noodles, and sauce. Mix gently until combined, being careful not to break up tofu.

Transfer to a large serving platter and top with chives and cilantro. Serve with Thai Cucumber Salad.

## Thai Cucumber Salad

- ¼ **cup sugar**
- ¼ **cup water**
- 2 **English cucumbers, unpeeled, rinsed, and dried**
- 1 **shallot**
- 2 **cloves garlic**
- ¼ **cup white vinegar**
  **Kosher salt**
  **Red pepper flakes**
- 2 **tablespoons coarsely chopped cilantro**
- 2 **tablespoons coarsely chopped dry roasted salted peanuts**

In a small saucepan, mix sugar and water together and bring to a boil. Cook, stirring, just until sugar dissolves, about 1 to 2 minutes. Remove from heat and let cool for 5 minutes.

While simple syrup is cooling, prepare vegetables: Quarter cucumbers lengthwise and slice to form triangles. Finely chop shallot and mince garlic.

Place cucumbers, shallots, and garlic in a medium bowl. Toss with simple syrup, vinegar, and salt and red pepper to taste.

Sprinkle with cilantro and peanuts.

. . . . . . . . . . . . . . . . . . . . . . . . . . . . . . . . . . . . . . . .

**Recommended Wine:**
**Gamla Sauvignon Blanc**

Asian-inspired dishes such as these are bursting with flavor and spice. They generally do best with a crisp, palate-cleansing white wine (still or sparkling).

# { Vietnamese Beef and Noodle Soup }

## Vietnamese Beef and Noodle Soup

*This recipe is inspired by a Vietnamese soup called "pho." The meat isn't cooked on a stove but when it is served. The boiling broth is poured over paper-thin strips of beef and the heat of the broth cooks it. Freeze the meat until firm, about 1 hour, to make slicing easier.*

1   (1-pound) box angel hair

1   tablespoon canola oil

2   cloves garlic, sliced

1   (32-ounce) box Manischewitz **All Natural Beef Broth**

2   (32-ounce) boxes Manischewitz **Reduced Sodium All Natural Chicken Broth**

1   star anise

½   teaspoon ground cinnamon

1   cube frozen **Gefen Crushed Garlic**

1   cube frozen crushed ginger

1   pound **New York** boneless strip steak, frozen for 1 hour

2   cups shredded lettuce

1   jalapeño, seeded and minced

¼   cup torn fresh cilantro leaves

     Lime wedges

Prepare pasta according to package instructions.

Heat oil in a 4- or 5-quart saucepan over medium-high heat. Fry garlic for about 1 minute until fragrant and golden. Transfer to a small bowl and set aside.

In the same pan, heat broths with star anise, cinnamon, and frozen garlic and ginger. Bring to a gentle boil and cook for 10 minutes.

While broth is cooking, slice beef: Using a mandoline or sharp knife, slice the steak, across the grain, very thin (about ⅛-inch).

Evenly distribute angel hair, lettuce, jalapeño, fried garlic, and beef among four large soup bowls. Pour broth into bowls, pushing beef into hot liquid so that it cooks. Top with cilantro and serve with lime wedges.

181

. . . . . . . . . . . . . . . . . . . . . . . . . . . . . . . . . . . .

**Recommended Wine:**
**Herzog Reserve Late Harvest Zinfandel**

Steak and cabernet sauvignon are a classic pairing. But, given the texture of the soup and the variety of the herbs and spices, you may want to get creative and try a red dessert wine.

# {If You've Got 60 Minutes}

When I got married, I was told that an opportune time to storm the Heavens with your prayers is while under the *chupah*. So picture this: I'm walking round and round my groom, desperately trying to cover all the important bases: health, our children-to-be, *shidduchim* for my friends, world peace—and food.

Yes, I may be the only bride in Jewish history to have fervently prayed under the *chupah* that even though I had never cooked anything in my life, somehow I would be transformed into a savvy *balabusta*. I was smart enough to know that I needed a miracle—that G-d had to smile on me in a very big way if my husband was ever to eat anything edible from my hands.

I'm happy to report that Divine intervention did arrive, and just in the nick of time: Not for my first *Shabbos* meal—which was a disaster—but shortly after. And like most miracles, it took a lot of work on my part to make it happen. I poured out my heart and soul through tears and prayers like all women since the beginning of time, but I was firmly focused on soups and salads, not to mention meat and potatoes.

So I thank G-d a million and one times for the fact that we survived our first year of culinary experimentation, and that I even learned enough to write cookbooks! Whoever thinks that G-d has no sense of irony has never been in my kitchen.

But that doesn't mean I've stopped praying. Quite the contrary—I feel that my culinary success is based more on my earnest invocations than anything else. *Erev Shabbos*, as I knead my challah, prepare our upcoming meals and even during candle-lighting, I beseech G-d to have mercy on my family and guests and let my food enhance the *Shabbos* experience in our home.

My five-year-old calls me "The Best Cooker Ever." Of course, my competition is mainly frozen kiddie favorites—pizza, chicken nuggets and fries—but I would still say that I'm doing ok! It turns out that with a little flair (bolstered by some creative prayers) it doesn't take much to make crowd pleasers.

If you have the time—let's say an hour—you have the luxury of experimenting with a new recipe, or trying something a wee bit more complex than the quickies. Let me give you a few examples off the top of my Cordon Bleu head: Chicken Pot Pie with Herb Dropped Biscuits or Seared Cod with Caramelized Onions are alot easier to prepare than they sound. (Serve the cod with Pan-Roasted Potato Chips and watch everyone go wild.) Or what about a hearty Irish Stew or Individual Meat Loaves with Wasabi Mashed Potatoes? Way out of the burgers and fries league, my friend. These are meals that both kids and adults will eat up in a flash.

Recipes for these easy, fun dishes—and more!—are in the following pages. So if you've got an hour till the dinner bell, think of it as plenty of time to prepare a feast for a king—or at least for your tableful of little princes and princesses!

{60} minute meals

# { Beef Bourguignon with Noodles }
## Salad with Apples and Walnuts

**Serves 6** | While beef is stewing, prepare Salad with Apples and Walnuts. Cook the noodles toward the end of the stewing time so the noodles will be hot when you serve them.

## Beef Bourguignon with Noodles

*This is a classic French dish that the whole family will enjoy. Having your butcher cube the beef for you saves you tons of time in the kitchen. Using silver tip beef eliminates the need for slow cooking.*

2   **tablespoons canola oil**

1   **½ pounds beef silver tip, in 1-inch cubes**

1   **(8-ounce) package baby bella mushrooms, quartered**

1   **(9-ounce) bag frozen white pearl onions, not thawed**

2   **medium carrots, peeled and sliced**

2   **tablespoons flour**

1   **(32-ounce) box Manischewitz All Natural Beef Broth**

½   **cup recommended red wine (see below)**

1   **teaspoon freshly ground black pepper**

¼   **cup fresh thyme leaves**

1   **(1-pound) package wide noodles**

Heat oil in a large heavy-bottomed saucepan or Dutch oven over medium-high heat. Pat beef very dry with paper towels so the beef will brown, not steam. Brown beef on all sides, about 5 minutes. Remove with a slotted spoon and set aside. Add mushrooms, onions, and carrots, scraping down the brown bits from the pan, stirring occasionally, for about 5 minutes. Sprinkle in flour, stir to mix and coat veggies. Add broth, wine, pepper, and thyme; return beef to the pan along with any accumulated juices. Bring to a boil, reduce heat to medium-low. Cook, uncovered, for 45 minutes, stirring occasionally.

While beef is stewing, prepare noodles according to package instructions. Drain and place in a serving bowl.

Spoon stew over noodles and serve with Salad with Apples and Walnuts.

## Salad with Apples and Walnuts

1   **(5-ounce) package mixed greens, rinsed and dried**

1   **apple, cored and thinly sliced**

½   **cup halved walnuts**

¾   **cup Basic Vinaigrette (see recipe page 43)**

Place mixed greens, apples, and walnuts in a salad bowl. Gently toss with vinaigrette.

**Recommended Wine:
Yatir Cabernet Sauvignon**

These delectable beef cubes deserve the king of red wine, cabernet sauvignon. TIP: Cook your meat in the same wine you will serve with the meal.

# { Chicago-Style Hot Dogs }
## Shoestring French Fries

. . . . . . . . . . . . . . . . . . . . . . . . . . . . . . . . . . . . . . . . . . . . . . . . . . . . . . . . . . . . . . . . . . . . . . . . .

**Serves 4**

## Chicago-Style Hot Dogs

*The Shake Shack in NYC is all the rage. Here is my very own kosher version of their Chicago Hot Dog.*

- 8   beef hot dogs
- 8   hot dog buns
- 1   on-the-vine tomato, coarsely chopped
- ½   medium red onion, coarsely chopped
- ½   English cucumber, quartered lengthwise, then sliced
- 1   kosher dill pickle, finely chopped
- ½   tablespoon poppy seeds
- ½   tablespoon celery salt
-     Sweet relish
-     Yellow mustard

Cook hot dogs according to package instructions.

In a medium bowl, mix tomatoes, onions, cucumbers, pickles, poppy seeds, and celery salt.

Place the buns on a serving platter. Place a hot dog on each bun with 2 tablespoons of the tomato mixture, and relish and mustard to taste.

Serve with Shoestring French Fries.

### Warm Rolls

*You can warm the buns by wrapping them in a damp paper towel and microwaving for about 10 seconds, steaming them briefly in a vegetable steamer, or lightly toasting them in your oven.*

## Shoestring French Fries

*The best French fries are the ones that are fried twice.*

- 6   large baking potatoes, peeled and cut into shoestrings (¼ x 4-inches), about 3 ½ pounds
- 2   cups canola oil
- 2   tablespoons kosher salt

Line a cookie sheet with paper towels.

Peel the potatoes and cut them into shoestrings on a mandoline.

Heat the oil over medium heat in a heavy-bottomed pan to 325° F. You can measure this with a deep-fry thermometer, or try dropping a cube of bread into the oil. If it is brown in 15 seconds, the oil is at the correct temperature.

Place the fries in the oil and cook for 3 to 4 minutes. Remove with a slotted spoon and place on the prepared cookie sheet to drain and cool.

Increase the heat of the oil to 375° F. Place the fries back in for 3 to 5 minutes or until golden brown. Remove with slotted spoon. Salt the fries and serve.

. . . . . . . . . . . . . . . . . . . . . . . . . . . . . . . . . . . . . .

**Recommended Wine:**
**Herzog Selection**
**Blanc de Blanc Brut Sparkling Wine**

Nothing goes with a hot dog as well as a beer; but for our wine-pairing recommendations, you can try a comparable sparkling wine.

# { Chicken Pot Pie with Herbed Drop Biscuits }

**Serves 8**

## Chicken Pot Pie with Herbed Drop Biscuits

*"Drop biscuit" literally means you just drop the batter by spoonfuls and bake them as opposed to a biscuit dough that you roll and cut. A drop biscuit is a traditional topping for a pot pie.*

For pot pie:

- 1 tablespoon canola oil
- 1 pound boneless, skinless chicken thighs, cut in bite-size pieces
- 2 teaspoons kosher salt, divided
- 1 medium onion, coarsely chopped
- 2 cups Manischewitz All Natural Chicken Broth
- 2 stalks celery, sliced
- 2 carrots, peeled and sliced into rounds
- 2 large potatoes, peeled and cut in bite-size chunks
- 1 sprig fresh thyme leaves or ½ teaspoon dried
- 1 teaspoon freshly ground black pepper
- 1 box frozen peas, not thawed

For biscuits:

- 2 cups flour
- 1 tablespoon baking powder
- 1 teaspoon kosher salt
- 4 tablespoons chopped fresh chives
- ¼ cup pareve margarine or shortening
- 1 large egg, beaten
- ½ cup soy milk

Preheat oven to 400° F. Grease a 3-quart casserole dish.

Over medium-high heat, heat oil in a sauté pan large enough to hold all ingredients. Season chicken with 1 teaspoon salt. Brown chicken in oil about 3 to 4 minutes on each side; transfer to a platter.

Add onions to the pan and cook for 5 minutes. Add chicken broth, bring to boil. Stir in celery, carrots, potatoes, thyme, remaining 1 teaspoon salt, and pepper. Cover and continue to cook for 10 minutes. Add chicken and peas; mix well. Cover and cook for 5 minutes more.

While the chicken and vegetables are cooking, make the biscuits: In a large bowl, whisk together flour, baking powder, salt, and chives. Using your fingertips, rub margarine into dry ingredients until mixture looks like crumbs. Do it quickly so the fats don't melt. Add egg and soy milk and stir vigorously with a wooden spoon until mixture comes together.

Transfer the chicken vegetable mixture to the prepared casserole dish. Drop the biscuit dough in 8 large spoonfuls on top of chicken mixture.

Bake for 20 minutes or until biscuits are golden brown.

## Herbed Crust

*If you want a crust to cover the entire pie, use 2/3 cup soy milk in the biscuit recipe; spread batter over the top and bake at 450° F for 20 to 25 minutes.*

**Recommended Wine:**
**Les Nosroyes Puligny Montrachet White Burgundy (Chardonnay)**

The doughy herbed biscuits would go great with a yeasty chardonnay. Try to find a French chardonnay prepared "Sur Lie" (on the yeast cells).

# { Greek-Style Chicken with Lemon and Dill }
## Tomatoes and String Beans

· · · · · · · · · · · · · · · · · · · · · · · · · · · · · · · · · · · · · · · · · · · · · ·

**Serves 6**

## Greek-Style Chicken with Lemon and Dill

2   **pounds boneless, skinless chicken breasts**

1   **tablespoon kosher salt**

1   **teaspoon freshly ground black pepper**

3   **tablespoons olive oil**

1   **large onion, coarsely chopped**

2   **carrots, peeled and julienned**

1   **stalk celery, trimmed and sliced**

¾   **cup cold water, divided**

2   **tablespoons chopped fresh dill**

1   **tablespoon cornstarch**

2   **large eggs**

½   **cup freshly squeezed lemon juice**

Season chicken with salt and pepper. Heat oil in a large saucepan over medium-high heat; and cook chicken breasts about 2 minutes on each side. Do not brown. Stir in onions, carrots, celery, ½ cup water, and dill. Cover and let cook for 10 minutes. Transfer chicken to a serving platter and set aside.

In a small bowl, mix cornstarch with remaining ¼ cup water until completely dissolved. Add cornstarch mixture to the sauce. Cook over low heat until thickened, about 2 minutes.

In a small bowl, beat eggs with lemon juice until frothy. Take a ladleful of the sauce and pour it slowly into the eggs, beating as you pour. Pour the egg mixture into the pan and cook over medium heat for about 5 minutes, stirring occasionally, until sauce thickens.

Pour sauce over the chicken breasts and serve immediately with Tomatoes and String Beans.

## Tomatoes and String Beans

1   **tablespoon olive oil**

1   **small onion, coarsely chopped**

1   **pound of fresh string beans, trimmed, or frozen, not thawed**

1   **(28-ounce) can chopped tomatoes, undrained**

2   **cloves garlic, minced**

2   **teaspoons kosher salt**

1   **teaspoon freshly ground black pepper**

In a saucepan, heat oil over medium heat. Add onions and let cook for 5 minutes. Add string beans, tomatoes, garlic, salt, and pepper. Cover and cook for 10 minutes if using frozen string beans, 20 minutes if using fresh. Taste and adjust seasonings, if needed.

· · · · · · · · · · · · · · · · · · · · · · · · · · · · · · · · · · · · ·

**Recommended Wine:**
**Goose Bay Viognier**

This creamy sauce can use a medium-bodied white. Try a Viognier whose floral aromas will complement the julienned vegetables and dill.

# { Individual Meat Loaves }
## Wasabi Mashed Potatoes

. . . . . . . . . . . . . . . . . . . . . . . . . . . . . . . . . . . . . . . . . . . . . . . . . . . . . . .

**Serves 4** | Prepare Wasabi Mashed Potatoes while meat loaves are baking.

## Individual Meat Loaves

**Gefen Canola Oil Cooking Spray**
1 tablespoon canola oil
1 medium onion, finely chopped
½ green pepper, seeds and ribs removed, finely chopped
1 pound ground beef
1 large egg, beaten
½ cup plain bread crumbs
¼ cup matzoh meal
1 ½ teaspoons kosher salt
1 teaspoon freshly ground black pepper
1 teaspoon dried thyme leaves
1 tablespoon Worcestershire sauce (see note page 245)
1 clove garlic, minced

Preheat oven to 425° F. Lightly spray 4 (6-ounce) ramekins with cooking spray.

In a small sauté pan, heat oil over medium heat and cook onions and peppers for 6 to 7 minutes.

While vegetables are cooking, combine ground beef, egg, bread crumbs, matzoh meal, salt, pepper, thyme, and Worcestershire sauce in a large bowl.

Add garlic to vegetables and cook for about 1 minute.

Add vegetables to the ground beef mixture and mix until combined.

Form into 4 balls and place in prepared ramekins. Place ramekins on a cookie sheet. Bake for 25 minutes.

Serve in the ramekins with Wasabi Mashed Potatoes on the side.

## Wasabi Mashed Potatoes

6 medium Yukon gold potatoes, peeled and quartered
2 cloves garlic
1 tablespoon kosher salt
¼ cup Manischewitz All Natural Vegetable Broth
4 tablespoons pareve margarine
2 tablespoons wasabi horseradish

In a large saucepan, boil potatoes and garlic in salted water. Cook for 15 to 20 minutes or until potatoes are tender and break apart with a fork. Drain and return to pan.

With a potato masher or hand mixer, mash potatoes and garlic with broth, margarine, and horseradish. Season with additional salt, if desired.

. . . . . . . . . . . . . . . . . . . . . . . . . . . . . . . . . . . .

**Recommended Wine:
Domaine Saint Benoit "Laureline"
Chateauneuf du Pape**

Though this version of the good old "meat and potatoes" is certainly fine cuisine, it will still pair nicely with a hearty red wine, such as one from the famed French "Chateauneuf du Pape."

# {Irish Stew}

............................................................................................

**Serves 8**

## Irish Stew

*Irish soda bread is a quick bread made with baking soda and raisins. If you can't find a kosher version, then serve this with biscuits or a raisin challah for a fun twist.*

2   tablespoons canola oil

2   pounds cubed tender beef chuck, in 1-inch pieces

1   tablespoon kosher salt

1   teaspoon freshly ground black pepper

2   cups baby carrots

3   medium onions, peeled and quartered

2   (32-ounce) boxes Manischewitz All Natural Chicken Broth

2   pounds red-skinned potatoes, unpeeled, scrubbed

¼   cup snipped fresh chives

Heat oil over high heat in a heavy-bottomed large saucepan or Dutch oven. Season meat with salt and pepper; add meat to the pan. Cook until browned, turning often, about 8 to 10 minutes. Transfer to a bowl when done.

Add carrots and onions to the pan and cook until brown, 3 to 5 minutes. Return meat to the pan and mix together. Add the broth and potatoes to the pan and bring to a boil. Turn heat down to a high simmer, cover, and let cook for 30 to 35 minutes, or until potatoes are cooked through and fork tender.

Stir in chives and serve with a bread of your choice.

## What is Irish Stew?

*Irish stew, like most traditional stews, is a hearty dish– perfect for those meat-and-potatoes men (or women and children) in your life. Traditionally made with lamb or beef, the telltale sign that you're eating an Irish stew is that the meat has not been browned. Browning the meat would be oh-so-untraditional in Ireland.*

............................................

**Recommended Wine:**
**Barkan Reserve Barrel Aged Pinotage**

This stew has the meat to hold up to a red wine and its rich flavors might make it just the dish to experiment with an unusual varietal—pinotage (a cross between the French pinot noir and cinsaut).

# {Lentil Dal with Chicken and Jasmine Rice}

**Serves 4**

## Lentil Dal with Chicken and Jasmine Rice

*For a different texture, you can purée half the lentils in a blender or food processor until smooth. Return the purée to the saucepan and mix well.*

- **4 boneless, skinless chicken breasts, about 1 pound**
- **½ cup freshly squeezed lemon juice**
- **1 tablespoon lemon zest**
- **1 tablespoon kosher salt**
- **1 teaspoon freshly ground black pepper**
- **1 ½ cups red lentils**
- **1 teaspoon turmeric**
- **1 teaspoon ground cumin**
- **½ teaspoon grated fresh ginger**
- **1 ½ cups jasmine rice**
- **2 tablespoons canola oil**
- **1 large onion, coarsely chopped**
- **3 cloves garlic, minced**
- **¼ cup whole fresh cilantro leaves**

Preheat oven to 400° F.

Place chicken in a resealable plastic bag with lemon juice, zest, salt, and pepper. Marinate for 10 minutes, turning once or twice.

In a medium saucepan, combine 4 cups water, lentils, turmeric, cumin, and ginger; bring to a boil. Reduce heat to simmer, cover, and cook for 10 to 12 minutes, or until lentils are done.

While lentils are cooking, prepare rice according to package instructions.

While rice is cooking, heat oil in a large sauté pan over medium heat. Add onions and cook for 5 minutes; add garlic and continue cooking for 1 minute more. Push onions to the sides of the pan; add chicken and brown evenly over medium heat, about 8 minutes on each side.

Plate lentils, top with chicken, sprinkle with cilantro. Serve with jasmine rice on the side.

**Recommended Wine: Gamla White Riesling**

The low-fat chicken breasts combined with the strong flavors imparted from the ginger, cumin, and turmeric call for a versatile white wine.

# {Mediterranean Frittata}
## Crisp Pita Chips with Hummus

. . . . . . . . . . . . . . . . . . . . . . . . . . . . . . . . . . . . . . . . . . . . . . . . . . . . . . . . . . . . . . . . . . .

**Serves 4** | Prepare pita chips while frittata is baking.

## Mediterranean Frittata

*This dish is also great the next day—*
*cold, straight out of the fridge.*

2  tablespoons butter

1  medium red onion, coarsely chopped

1  medium red pepper, seeds and ribs removed,
   coarsely chopped

10  large eggs

1  tablespoon kosher salt

1  teaspoon cracked black pepper

¼  cup chopped fresh basil

⅓  cup crumbled feta

Preheat oven to 375° F.

Melt butter in a 10-inch ovenproof sauté pan over
medium heat.

Cook onions and peppers in butter for 5 minutes,
stirring occasionally.

In a large bowl, beat eggs with salt, pepper, and basil.
Pour egg mixture into the pan. Cook until edges start
to set, about 3 minutes. Sprinkle feta over eggs.

Transfer pan to the oven and bake for 25 minutes.
Using a pot holder, shake the pan to make sure the egg
mixture is set and is no longer moving. Frittata will puff
up and be slightly brown on top when it is done.

Let the frittata cool in the pan on a wire rack for about
10 minutes. Place a plate over the top of the pan and
invert the frittata onto the plate. Cut into wedges.
Serve at room temperature with Crisp Pita Chips
with Hummus.

## Crisp Pita Chips with Hummus

   **Olive oil**

4  **pitas**

1  **(10-ounce) container hummus**

Heat about 1 inch of oil in a large sauté pan over
medium heat.

On a cutting board, stack pitas and cut into eighths with
a sharp bread knife.

Fry pita chips in hot oil for 2 to 4 minutes. Pitas should
be lightly browned and crisp. Be careful not to crowd
the pan or the pitas won't crisp; you may need to work
in batches, adding and heating more oil as needed.

Spoon hummus into a small serving bowl placed in the
middle of a large platter. Surround bowl with pita chips.

. . . . . . . . . . . . . . . . . . . . . . . . . . . . . . . . . . . . . . .

**Recommended Wine:**
**Baron Herzog Sauvignon Blanc**

This egg-based dish is light and flavorful and
should be accompanied by a light wine, such as
a sauvignon blanc, that will cleanse the palate
between bites.

# { Muffuletta }

## Strawberry Lemonade

. . . . . . . . . . . . . . . . . . . . . . . . . . . . . . . . . . . . . . . . . . . . . . . . . . . . . . . . . . . . . . . . . . . . . . . . .

**Serves 6** I While Muffuletta is baking, prepare Strawberry Lemonade.

## Muffuletta

*Muffuletta is a sandwich that originated in New Orleans. Legend has it that Salvatore Lupo of Central Grocery had olives left over from the bottom of the barrel and invented this famous sandwich to use them up. Here is a kosher take on it.*

**Gefen Canola Oil Cooking Spray**

I **(10-ounce) jar stuffed manzanilla olives, drained and finely chopped**

I **(10-ounce) jar roasted red pepper strips, drained and finely chopped**

I **medium red onion, finely chopped**

2 **stalks celery, finely chopped**

½ **cup extra virgin olive oil, divided**

¼ **cup red wine vinegar**

I **tablespoon dried oregano**

I **teaspoon kosher salt**

I **teaspoon freshly ground black pepper**

I **(16-ounce) package frozen bread dough, thawed**

I **pound sliced smoked turkey, divided**

½ **pound sliced salami, divided**


Preheat oven to 375° F. Lightly spray 2 jelly-roll pans with cooking spray.

In a medium bowl, combine olives, peppers, onions, celery, ¼ cup olive oil, vinegar, oregano, salt, and pepper. Mix together and set aside.

On a lightly floured work surface, divide bread dough in half. Take one of the pieces of dough and roll it out to a 9- x 13-inch rectangle. Transfer dough to a prepared pan.

Lay one-half of the turkey over half of the dough, lengthwise. Lay one-half of the salami over the turkey. Drain the olive salad and spread one-half of it over the salami. Fold the dough over to cover the filling, and seal the edges by pressing them together with a fork or your fingers.

Repeat with the remaining bread dough and ingredients on the second prepared pan. Brush both muffulettas with remaining ¼ cup olive oil.

With a sharp knife, make slits about 2 inches apart in the tops of the muffulettas. Bake for 30 minutes. Remove from oven; let cool briefly. Cut into thirds and serve with Strawberry Lemonade.

## Strawberry Lemonade

I **cup sugar**

4 **cups cold water, divided**

I **cup freshly squeezed lemon juice**

I **cup frozen strawberries, not thawed**


In a small saucepan over medium heat, mix sugar with I cup water and cook, stirring, until sugar dissolves. Put sugar syrup, lemon juice, and strawberries in a pitcher and dilute with remaining 3 cups water. Stir well.

Serve over ice.

. . . . . . . . . . . . . . . . . . . . . . . . . . . . . . . . . . . . . . . .

**Recommended Wine:
Goose Bay Pinot Noir**

While the salami and smoked turkey might bring a smoky red wine to mind, the vinegar, onion, olives, and peppers probably require a wine with fewer tannins and greater acidity.

# { Nachos with the Works }
## Pumpkin Black Bean Soup

. . . . . . . . . . . . . . . . . . . . . . . . . . . . . . . . . . . . . . . . . . . . . . . . . . . . . . . . . . . . . . . . . . . .

**Serves 4 to 6** | While the soup is cooking, prepare the nachos.

## Nachos with the Works

½  **cup instant rice**

   **Gefen Canola Oil Cooking Spray**

For nachos:

1  **(9-ounce) bag yellow or blue tortilla chips**

1  **small red pepper, seeds and ribs removed, coarsely chopped**

½  **medium onion, coarsely chopped**

1  **(15-ounce) can black beans, rinsed and drained**

2  **cups shredded Les Petites Fermieres Colby Jack, divided**

1  **jalapeño pepper, halved, seeded and thinly sliced**

For guacamole:

3  **ripe avocados**

   **Freshly squeezed juice of 1 lime**

1  **teaspoon chopped fresh cilantro**

1  **tablespoon finely chopped onion**

¼  **cup finely chopped tomatoes**

½  **teaspoon kosher salt**

1  **(12-ounce) jar prepared salsa, for serving**

1  **(8-ounce) container sour cream, for serving**

Prepare rice according to package instructions and set aside.

Preheat oven to 350° F. Lightly spray a 17- x 11-inch baking sheet or large ovenproof serving platter with cooking spray. Spread chips on the prepared baking sheet. It's okay if the chips overlap.

In a bowl, combine, peppers, onions, black beans, and rice. Spoon evenly over chips. Top with cheese and jalapeños. Bake for 10 minutes, rotating pan halfway through.

Cut avocados in half, remove pits, and scoop flesh out into a bowl. Mash avocado and mix in lime juice, cilantro, onions, tomatoes, and salt. Set aside.

Serve nachos hot with guacamole, salsa, and sour cream on the side along with Pumpkin Black Bean Soup.

## Pumpkin Black Bean Soup

*This soup has a kick from the cayenne—adjust the heat to your liking.*

2  **tablespoons olive oil**

1  **small onion, coarsely chopped**

1  **small green pepper, seeds and ribs removed, coarsely chopped**

2  **cloves garlic, minced**

1  **(15-ounce) can puréed pumpkin, or 2 (12-ounce) boxes frozen cooked winter squash, thawed**

1  **(32-ounce) box Manischewitz All Natural Vegetable Broth**

1  **teaspoon ground cumin**

1  **tablespoon kosher salt**

1  **tablespoon cayenne pepper**

1  **(15 ½-ounce) can black beans, rinsed and drained**

1  **tablespoon chopped fresh cilantro**

1  **(8-ounce) container regular or low-fat sour cream**

In a 4-quart pot, heat olive oil over medium heat and cook onions and peppers until soft, about 5 minutes. Add garlic, stir, and continue cooking for 2 minutes more. Add pumpkin and broth. Stir until smooth. Add black beans, cumin, salt, and cayenne pepper; mix well. Cook, uncovered, over medium heat for 10 minutes.

With an immersion blender or in a food processor, purée about one-third of the soup and return the purée to the pot. Stir to combine.

Ladle into bowls. Garnish with cilantro and sour cream.

. . . . . . . . . . . . . . . . . . . . . . . . . . . . . . . . . . . . . . .

**Recommended Wine:**
**Bartenura Prosecco Brut**

Jalapeño peppers, black beans, Colby Jack cheese, pumpkin—an explosive array of flavors likely to clash with traditional wines. A bottle of bubbly is your best bet!

# { Orange Honey Mustard Roasted Chicken }

## Garlic Roasted Brussels Sprouts

. . . . . . . . . . . . . . . . . . . . . . . . . . . . . . . . . . . . . . . . . . . . . . . . . . . . . . . . . . . . . . . . . . . . . . . . . . . . . . . . .

**Serves 4** | Put both dishes in the oven at the same time and they'll be ready to serve together.

## Orange Honey Mustard Roasted Chicken

1   **small onion, coarsely chopped**

1   **stalk celery, cut in 2-inch chunks**

2   **sprigs parsley**

1   **(3-pound) chicken, cut in eighths**

½   **cup honey**

½   **cup Dijon mustard**

½   **cup store-bought orange juice**

2   **tablespoons orange zest**

Preheat oven to 450° F.

In a large roasting pan, place onions, celery, and parsley. Arrange chicken on top of vegetables.

In a small bowl, whisk together honey, mustard, orange juice, and zest. Pour the sauce over chicken and bake, covered, for 25 minutes. Reduce oven temperature to 425° F, uncover and roast for 10 minutes more, or until juices run clear when chicken is pierced with a fork.

Transfer to a serving platter and serve with Garlic Roasted Brussels Sprouts.

## Garlic Roasted Brussels Sprouts

2   **pounds frozen Brussels sprouts, not thawed**

¼   **cup olive oil**

1   **½ teaspoons kosher salt**

¾   **teaspoon freshly ground black pepper**

2   **cubes frozen Gefen Crushed Garlic, thawed**

Preheat oven to 450°F. Line a jelly-roll pan with foil.

In a large bowl, toss Brussels sprouts with oil, salt, pepper, and garlic. Place Brussels sprouts on prepared pan and roast for 25 minutes. Reduce heat to 425° F and roast for 10 minutes more, shaking the pan every once in a while.

207

. . . . . . . . . . . . . . . . . . . . . . . . . . . . . . . . . . . . . . . . . .

**Recommended Wine:**
**Psagot Merlot**

This sweet and tangy roasted chicken can stand up to a full-bodied red wine. But a fruity one will do best, as dry wines can taste bitter when paired with sweet foods.

# {Potato, Corn, and Cod Chowder}
## Homemade Biscuits

**Serves 6** | Yield 8 biscuits. Prepare biscuit dough. While the dough is chilling, prepare Potato, Corn, and Cod Chowder. Keep soup warm over low heat until biscuits are baked and serve together.

## Potato, Corn, and Cod Chowder

- 1 tablespoon canola oil
- 1 medium onion, finely chopped
- 1 pound red-skinned potatoes, scrubbed and cut in bite-size pieces
- 1 teaspoon kosher salt
- ½ teaspoon cracked black pepper
- 1 (32-ounce) box Manischewitz All Natural Vegetable Broth
- 1 teaspoon dried thyme leaves
- 2 cups heavy cream
- 1 (16-ounce) bag frozen corn, not thawed
- 1 pound cod filet, cut in 1-inch chunks

In an 8-quart stockpot, heat oil over medium heat. Add onions and cook for 5 minutes. Stir in potatoes, and season with salt and pepper. Cook for 5 minutes more. Add broth and thyme; mix well. Cover and bring to a boil. Reduce heat and simmer for 10 minutes. Stir in cream and corn.

Transfer about one-third of the soup to a mixing bowl and purée; return to the stockpot. Add cod without mixing. Cover and cook for about 7 minutes, or until cod is opaque and flakey. Adjust seasoning, if needed.

Serve hot with Homemade Biscuits.

## Homemade Biscuits

*Too much kneading can make the biscuits tough; so knead only until dough is pliable.*

- 2 cups flour plus more for kneading
- 1 tablespoon sugar
- ½ teaspoon kosher salt
- 2 teaspoons baking powder
- 5 tablespoons vegetable shortening
- ⅔ cup whole milk

Preheat oven to 450° F. Line a cookie sheet with parchment paper.

In a large bowl, mix flour, sugar, salt, and baking powder.

Using your fingertips, rub shortening into dry ingredients until mixture looks like crumbs. Do it quickly so the fats don't melt. Add milk and stir vigorously with a wooden spoon until mixture comes together. Turn out onto a floured board.

Knead for 2 minutes, adding flour as necessary to keep dough from being too sticky. Refrigerate for 30 minutes.

Using a rolling pin, roll out dough to ½-inch thickness. Cut into rounds with a 2 ½-inch diameter biscuit cutter or glass. Gather scraps; roll out again and cut more rounds.

Place biscuits on the prepared cookie sheet and bake for 10 minutes or until golden brown.

**Recommended Wine: Tzuba Chardonnay**

This hearty, comforting chowder can probably hold up to a red wine, but may do better with a full-bodied white.

# {Romanian Pizza}
## Tomato, Red Onion, and Sour Cream Salad

. . . . . . . . . . . . . . . . . . . . . . . . . . . . . . . . . . . . . . . . . . . . . . . . . . . . . . . . . . . . . . . . . . . . . . . . . .

**Serves 4** I While pizza is baking, prepare salad vegetables and dressing. Assemble the salad just before serving.

## Romanian Pizza

**Gefen Canola Oil Cooking Spray**
1   teaspoon canola oil
1   medium onion, coarsely chopped
2   cups Natural & Kosher Ricotta
1   cup Natural & Kosher Shredded Mozzarella
1   cup chopped dill
1   teaspoon kosher salt
1   teaspoon freshly ground black pepper
1   (16-ounce) package pizza dough
¼   cup flour
¼   cup olive oil

Preheat oven to 375° F. Lightly grease a jelly-roll pan with cooking spray.

In a small saucepan, heat oil over medium heat. Add onions and cook for 5 minutes or until soft.

In a large bowl, combine onions, ricotta, mozzarella, dill, salt, and pepper.

Divide pizza dough into 4 equal parts. On a floured board, stretch or press out each piece of dough to a circle about 8 inches in diameter. Distribute the ricotta filling evenly among the circles, placing the filling on one half of the dough. Fold each circle in half over the filling and seal the edges by pressing them together with a fork or your fingers. Brush with olive oil. Transfer to prepared cookie sheet and bake for 25 minutes.

Serve warm with Tomato, Red Onion, and Sour Cream Salad.

## Tomato, Red Onion, and Sour Cream Salad

3   on-the-vine tomatoes, thinly sliced
1   medium red onion, thinly sliced
1   teaspoon kosher salt
1   cup regular or low-fat sour cream
1   teaspoon freshly squeezed lemon juice
2   teaspoons snipped chives
    **Freshly ground black pepper**

Arrange tomatoes with onions on a shallow plate. Season with salt.

In a small bowl, combine sour cream with lemon juice and chives. Spoon over tomatoes and onions, and season with pepper to taste.

. . . . . . . . . . . . . . . . . . . . . . . . . . . . . . . . . . . . . .

**Recommended Wine:
Hagafen Brut Cuvée**

Pizza with red sauce goes well with light red wines, but this white pizza brings to mind beer. Go for a nice Brut sparkling wine as a classy beverage option.

# { Seared Cod Filet with Caramelized Onions }
## Pan-Roasted Potato Chips

**Serves 4** | Prepare Pan-Roasted Potato Chips first.

## Seared Cod Filet with Caramelized Onions

- 4  tablespoons butter, divided
- 4  tablespoons canola oil, divided
- 1  large red onion, thinly sliced
- 1  large Vidalia onion, thinly sliced
- 1  tablespoon sugar
- ¼  cup packed dark brown sugar
- 2  teaspoons Gefen Coarse Sea Salt
- 1  teaspoon cracked black pepper
- ⅛  teaspoon ground cloves
- 4  (6-ounce) cod filets
-    Lemon wedges

Heat 2 tablespoons butter and 2 tablespoons oil in a large heavy-bottomed sauté pan over medium heat. Add onions; stir in (white) sugar. Cook, stirring often to prevent burning, for 30 minutes or until onions are browned and caramelized.

While onions are cooking, mix together brown sugar, salt, pepper, and cloves on a flat plate.

Heat remaining 2 tablespoons butter and remaining 2 tablespoons oil in a second large sauté pan. Press brown sugar mixture onto both sides of each filet. Gently place in the pan and cook over medium heat for about 7 minutes. Turn carefully and continue cooking for another 5 minutes, or until fish is opaque and flakes easily with a fork.

Place fish on a platter and top with caramelized onions. Serve with lemon wedges and Pan-Roasted Potato Chips.

## Pan-Roasted Potato Chips

*Using a mandoline will give you uniform slices for uniform cooking. Placing the sliced potatoes in cold water prevents oxidization and removes starch, resulting in a crispier chip.*

-    Canola oil for frying
- 2  russet potatoes, unpeeled and scrubbed
-    Kosher salt
-    Freshly ground black pepper

Preheat oven to 275° F.

Slice potatoes about ⅛-inch thick. As you slice, place potatoes into a large bowl filled with cold water. Before frying, lay potatoes on paper towels and pat very dry.

Pour 1 inch of oil into a large heavy-bottomed sauté pan. Heat oil over medium heat to 375° F.

Working in batches: When oil is shimmering, add potatoes in a single layer and cook for about 5 minutes, or until bottoms are browned. Turn and continue cooking for another 3 minutes. Transfer to a baking pan. Sprinkle with salt and pepper to taste and keep warm in the oven while cooking remaining potatoes.

**Recommended Wine:**
**Carmel Ridge Red (blend)**

White flaky fish such as cod can clash with red wine and make it taste metallic. Here, however, the cod is dredged in a brown sugar mixture that will make it a nice match for red wine. Try picking a light, fruity red wine.

# {Smoked Salmon Crêpes}
## Israeli Salad with Dill

. . . . . . . . . . . . . . . . . . . . . . . . . . . . . . . . . . . . . . . . . . . . . . . . . . . . . . . .

**Serves 8** | Yield 24 crêpes

## Smoked Salmon Crêpes

2   **cups flour**

1   **teaspoon kosher salt**

4   **large eggs, lightly beaten**

½   **cup canola oil, divided**

1   **(12-ounce) container regular or low-fat sour cream**

24   **slices smoked salmon, about 2 ½ pounds**

1   **medium red onion, thinly sliced**

½   **cup capers, drained**

¼   **cup chopped fresh chives**

In a large bowl, whisk flour with salt. Whisk in eggs. Slowly add 2 cups water in a continuous stream, whisking continually until you have a thin batter. Chill in refrigerator for 15 minutes.

To make crêpes: Lay out paper towels on a work surface. Heat 1 tablespoon oil in a 6-inch sauté pan over medium heat. Do not use too much oil, just enough to make sure the pan is coated. Pour ¼ cup batter in the center of the pan and, tilting the pan, swirl the batter to the edges. As soon as the bottom is cooked, about 45 seconds, transfer crêpe to paper towels by sliding it out with a spatula or inverting the pan. You can stack the crêpes if you separate them with waxed paper, otherwise they will stick together. Repeat until all batter is used.

To assemble the crêpes: Spread a layer of sour cream on one side of each of the crêpes. Lay one slice smoked salmon on the sour cream. Sprinkle with onions. Roll up and place on a platter, seam-side down. Repeat until all crêpes and filling ingredients are used.

Sprinkle with capers and chopped chives. Serve with Israeli Salad with Dill.

## Israeli Salad with Dill

2   **tomatoes, coarsely chopped**

1   **English cucumber, unpeeled, rinsed, dried, and coarsely chopped**

1   **medium red onion, finely chopped**

1   **teaspoon kosher salt**

¼   **cup freshly squeezed lemon juice**

¼   **cup extra virgin olive oil**

¼   **cup chopped fresh dill**

In a medium serving bowl, combine tomatoes, cucumbers, and onions. Toss with salt.

In a small bowl, whisk together lemon juice, olive oil, and dill. Pour dressing over the vegetables. Toss and serve.

. . . . . . . . . . . . . . . . . . . . . . . . . . . . . . . . . . .

**Recommended Wine:**
**Binyamina Reserve**
**Unoaked Chardonnay**

Smoked salmon and sour cream really need a white wine. Try a crisp, unoaked chardonnay.

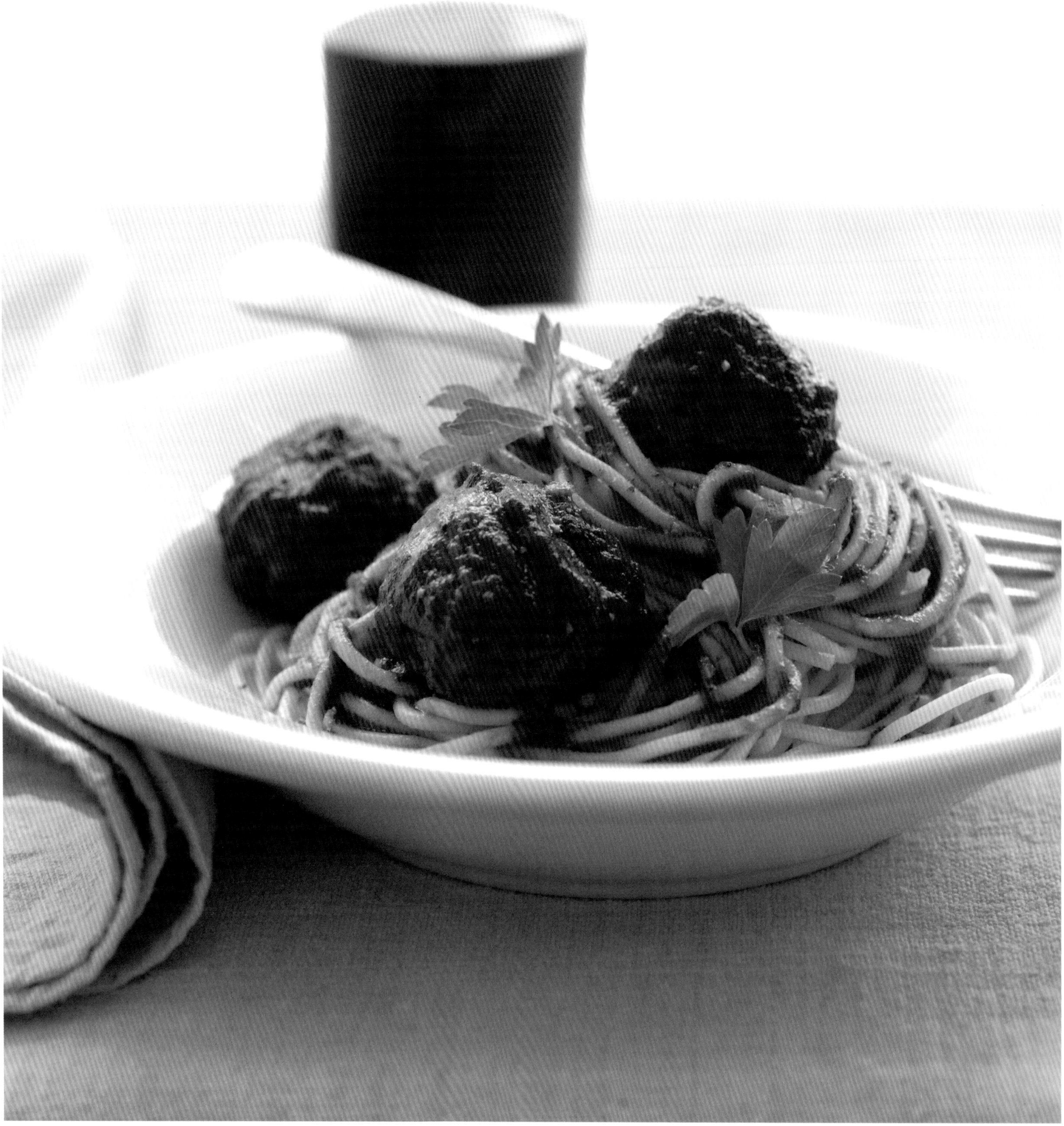

# { Spaghetti with Turkey Meatballs }

**Serves 4**

## Spaghetti with Turkey Meatballs

- 6 cups Gefen Classic Marinara Pasta Sauce
- 1 small onion, finely chopped
- 1 clove garlic, minced
- 1 pound ground turkey breast
- 1 teaspoon kosher salt
- 1 teaspoon freshly ground black pepper
- 1 large egg, beaten
- 1 cup plain bread crumbs
- ¼ cup finely chopped fresh parsley
- 1 tablespoon olive oil
- 1 (1-pound) box spaghetti
- 1 (5-ounce) package mixed greens
- ¾ cup bottled Italian dressing

In a 4-quart saucepot, warm sauce over medium-low heat.

In a medium bowl, combine onions, garlic, turkey, salt, pepper, egg, bread crumbs, and parsley. Form into 2-inch balls.

In a 12-inch skillet, heat olive oil over medium-high heat. Working in batches, add the meatballs to the skillet, browning on all sides, about 5 minutes.

Add the meatballs to the sauce and cook for 40 minutes. During the last 10 minutes of cooking, prepare pasta according to package instructions.

In a salad bowl, toss mixed greens with dressing.

Serve meatballs and sauce over spaghetti with salad on the side.

## The Ultimate Family Meal

*Spaghetti and meatballs are a family friendly favorite, at least in our house. For a change from the classic red meat dish, ground turkey or even chicken can still be crowd pleasers. The meatballs should not be tough and the perfect sauce is key to making this recipe the number one requested weeknight, Shabbos and holiday dish, no matter how old you are.*

217

**Recommended Wine:**
**Carmel Appellation Carignan**

Classic spaghetti and meatballs with a turkey twist. Try an earthy yet fruit-driven and complex wine from Israel.

# {Veal Scallopini with Tomato Chutney}

## Garlic Orzo with Peas

. . . . . . . . . . . . . . . . . . . . . . . . . . . . . . . . . . . . . . . . . . . . . . . . . . . . . . . .

**Serves 4** I While chutney is cooking, prepare Garlic Orzo with Peas.

## Veal Scallopini with Tomato Chutney

For veal:

½   **cup flour**

1 ½ **teaspoons kosher salt**

1   **teaspoon freshly ground black pepper**

8   **slices veal scallopini, about 1 ½ pounds**

2   **tablespoons olive oil**

For chutney:

1   **tablespoon olive oil**

1   **small onion, finely chopped**

1   **clove garlic, minced**

1   **(28-ounce) can diced tomatoes, undrained**

1   **tablespoon sugar**

1   **tablespoon red wine vinegar**

¼   **cup chopped fresh parsley**

In a pie plate or shallow bowl, mix together flour, salt, and pepper. Pat veal dry with paper towels and dredge in flour mixture. Heat oil in a 12-inch skillet over medium-high heat. When oil is hot, but not smoking, add veal, and cook until deep golden brown on both sides, about 5 minutes per side. Drain on paper towels.

In a large saucepan, heat oil over medium heat. Sauté onions in oil, stirring occasionally for about 5 minutes, or until soft. Add garlic, cook for 1 minute more. Stir in tomatoes, sugar, and vinegar. Cook, uncovered, stirring occasionally, for 15 minutes, or until chutney is thick. Stir in parsley just before serving.

Serve chutney over veal with Garlic Orzo with Peas.

## Garlic Orzo with Peas

1   ⅓ **cups orzo**

¼   **cup extra virgin olive oil**

1   **cup frozen peas, thawed**

3   **cloves garlic, minced**

Prepare orzo according to package instructions. Drain and place in a large serving bowl.

In a small saucepan, heat oil over medium heat for 1 to 2 minutes. Add garlic and peas and cook for 1 minute until garlic is fragrant. Toss with orzo and serve.

. . . . . . . . . . . . . . . . . . . . . . . . . . . . . . . . .

**Recommended Wine:**
**Herzog Reserve Edna Valley Syrah**

Veal is a meat with gamey flavors that has proven to pair wonderfully with the earthy and gamey characteristics of an old-world-style Syrah.

# { Vegetable Empanadas }
## Iced Mexican Coffee

......................................................................................................

**Serves 4** | Yield 4 empanadas. While empanadas are baking, prepare Iced Mexican Coffee.

## Vegetable Empanadas

- 1  tablespoon canola oil
- 1  small onion, finely chopped
- 1  clove garlic, minced
- 1  cup peeled (¼-inch) cubes butternut squash
   Kosher salt
- 1  cup canned black beans, rinsed and drained
- 1  (8 ¾-ounce) can yellow corn, drained
- ¼  cup raisins
- ¼  cup pitted black olives, drained and finely chopped
- 2  (14-ounce) packages refrigerated pie crusts

Preheat oven to 450° F. Line a jelly-roll pan with parchment paper.

In a medium sauté pan, heat oil over medium heat. Cook onions for 3 minutes; add garlic and cook for 2 minutes more, stirring occasionally. Remove from heat and transfer vegetables to a large bowl.

In the same pan, add ½ cup water, squash, and salt. Cover and cook over high heat for 5 minutes or until tender. Drain and place in the bowl with onions and garlic. Stir in black beans, corn, raisins, olives, and ½ teaspoon salt; mix thoroughly.

Divide the pie crust into 4 equal parts. On a floured board, stretch or press out each piece into a circle about 8 inches in diameter.

Spread equal amounts of filling on one-half of each circle. Fold the circle in half over the filling and crimp the edges with your fingers or a fork to seal well. You may need to use some water as a glue to secure the seal.

Place the empanadas on the prepared pan and bake for about 25 minutes, or until golden brown.

Serve with Iced Mexican Coffee.

## Iced Mexican Coffee

*If you allow the cinnamon sticks to steep for a few minutes in the hot coffee, the flavors will intensify and become even richer.*

- 4  cinnamon sticks
- ¼  cup packed brown sugar
- 32  ounces freshly brewed coffee
   Whipped cream

Place ice cubes and 1 cinnamon stick in each of 4 glasses.

Stir brown sugar into coffee. Pour 8 ounces of coffee into each glass. Top with whipped cream.

..........................................

**Recommended Wine:**
**Elvi Adar**

Black beans, black olives, and corn—masterfully blended into a scrumptious Spanish dish. Go for a rich Spanish red wine!

# { Vegetarian Chili }
## Homemade Corn Bread

. . . . . . . . . . . . . . . . . . . . . . . . . . . . . . . . . . . . . . . . . . . . . . . . . . . . . . . . . . . . . . . . .

Serves 6 | When chili is simmering, prepare Homemade Corn Bread.

## Vegetarian Chili

- 2 tablespoons canola oil
- 1 medium onion, coarsely chopped
- 1 green pepper, seeds and ribs removed, coarsely chopped
- 4 cloves garlic, minced
- 2 teaspoons chili powder
- 1 teaspoon ground cumin
- 1 ½ teaspoons kosher salt
- 1 (6-ounce) can tomato paste
- 1 tablespoon vinegar
- 1 (28-ounce) can diced tomatoes, undrained
- 2 (15-ounce) cans red kidney beans, rinsed and drained
- 1 (15-ounce) can pinto beans, rinsed and drained
- 2 cups water
- 1 teaspoon sugar
- 1 cinnamon stick
- 3 cups Les Petites Fermieres Shredded Cheddar

Heat oil in a large saucepan over medium-high heat. Cook onions and peppers for about 6 minutes. Stir in garlic, chili powder, cumin, salt, tomato paste, vinegar, tomatoes, beans, water, sugar, and cinnamon stick. Bring to a boil and reduce to medium heat. Simmer, uncovered, for 25 minutes, stirring occasionally.

Remove cinnamon stick before serving.

Spoon into individual bowls; top with cheddar cheese and serve with Homemade Corn Bread.

## Homemade Corn Bread

- Butter or margarine for greasing pan
- 1 cup yellow cornmeal
- 1 cup flour
- 1 tablespoon sugar
- 2 teaspoons baking powder
- ½ teaspoon baking soda
- ¼ teaspoon kosher salt
- 1 large egg
- 1 cup buttermilk
- 1 (11-ounce) can corn, drained
- 4 tablespoons butter or margarine, melted

Preheat oven to 375° F. Grease a 9-inch square pan.

In large bowl, whisk together cornmeal, flour, sugar, baking powder, baking soda, and salt.

In a small bowl, beat the egg and buttermilk. Stir the buttermilk mixture into the cornmeal mixture until smooth. Mix corn and butter into the batter.

Pour into prepared pan and bake for 20 to 25 minutes. Let cool for 5 minutes. Cut into squares before removing from pan.

. . . . . . . . . . . . . . . . . . . . . . . . . . . . . . . . . . . . . .

**Recommended Wine:**
**Segal's Fusion White**

The assortment of vegetables, spices, and cheddar cheese makes this dish a good pairing for a chilled and refreshing white wine.

# { Wild Mushroom Rigatoni }
## Lemon-Scented Broccoli Rabe

. . . . . . . . . . . . . . . . . . . . . . . . . . . . . . . . . . . . . . . . . . . . . . . . . . . . . . . . . . . . . . .

Serves 6

## Wild Mushroom Rigatoni

2  (1-ounce) packages dried wild mushrooms, rinsed and patted dry

1  cup Manischewitz All Natural Vegetable Broth

2  tablespoons dry sherry

1  (1-pound) box spelt or other rigatoni

1  (12-ounce) jar marinated and quartered artichoke hearts, drained, marinade reserved

2  cloves garlic, minced

1  (8-ounce) package sun-dried tomatoes, coarsely chopped

¼  cup olive oil

⅔  cup Natural & Kosher Grated Parmesan, plus additional for serving

In a bowl, soak mushrooms in vegetable broth and sherry for 10 minutes.

Cook rigatoni according to package instructions.

While rigatoni is cooking, heat artichoke marinade in a sauté pan over medium heat. Add garlic, sauté for 3 minutes.

Reserving the liquid, drain and coarsely chop mushrooms. Add mushrooms and sun-dried tomatoes to sauté pan and cook for 2 minutes. Add mushroom liquid and artichokes; heat through.

Toss cooked pasta with mushroom sauce, olive oil, and Parmesan.

Sprinkle additional Parmesan over top and serve with Lemon-Scented Broccoli Rabe.

## Lemon-Scented Broccoli Rabe

2  bunches broccoli rabe, about 2 pounds, coarsely chopped

¼  cup olive oil

2  tablespoons Gefen Coarse Sea Salt

1  tablespoon freshly ground black pepper

2  tablespoons freshly squeezed lemon juice

Rinse and dry the broccoli rabe. In a large sauté pan, heat olive oil over medium heat. Add broccoli rabe, tossing and stirring so that it cooks evenly. Continue cooking for 10 minutes, stirring occasionally so as not to burn.

Transfer the broccoli rabe to a serving bowl and season with salt and pepper. Toss to combine.

Sprinkle with lemon juice and serve.

. . . . . . . . . . . . . . . . . . . . . . . . . . . . . . . . . . . . . . . . .

**Recommended Wine:
Carmel Appellation Cabernet Sauvignon/Shiraz**

A hearty "comfort food" pasta dish like this will go nicely with a red wine blend that can stand up to the intense flavors of the dish.

# { For Special Days }

Ever since Sarah first set foot in Abraham's tent centuries ago, cooking for *Shabbos* and the holidays has been a Jewish pastime—ok, an obsession for some of us. For others, it's a creative passion—but it should *never* be a burden to anyone. Sarah wouldn't want that.

So if you're facing an upcoming holiday and your jaw is already tightening, my message to you is—*Don't panic!* Jamie is here! In this section, you'll find 10 complete holiday menus, with the recipes neatly laid out for you, all tied up with a ribbon. In record time, you'll have a fantabulous spread, fit for any visiting royalty (including the *Shabbos* Queen)—prepped, cooked, and ready to serve!

Let me give you a thumbnail sketch of what's to come: First, of course, is **Shabbos**. While I have no argument with tradition, I do get tired of serving the same meals every week and I figure you might be craving a little change too. We'll stick with the familiar fish, soup, meat concept—but how about striped bass or smoked trout for the fish course? Why not consider Pot au Feu instead of chulent for *Shabbos* lunch? That's just a sample, so fasten your seat belt!

Around **Rosh Hashanah** time, I go apple-picking with my kids (because Mommy just *loves* lifting her toddlers to reach the branches "just one more time"), and then let them help me use their apples in a special *Yuntif* recipe. Of course, there is a custom to eat honey and other sweet foods on this holiday, as well as *simanim*, foods whose names suggest a variety of blessings for the new year. These include pomegranates, leeks, beets, dates, and carrots —foods you may have been serving year round, but suddenly, they're in the spotlight, laden with symbolic promises of good things to come. In this section, we'll have fun seeing how many of these we can work into our Rosh Hashanah recipes.

Just before **Yom Kippur**, it's important to eat foods that make fasting easier—in fact, it's a *mitzvah*. First, you want to minimize salt and spices that may induce thirst. But that doesn't mean that the pre-Yom Kippur feast must be bland or boring! I'll give you a post-Yom Kippur meal too. It may not contain every dish you fantasized about during the fast, but it's sure to be satisfying.

It's an indescribable delight to sit in our *sukkah* on **Succos** in the back yard, watching the sunlight play off the decorations my kids so lovingly crafted. We always squeeze as many guests as we can into our little wooden palace. So if you have lots of company on this holiday too, surprise them by raiding ye olde Thanksgiving recipe box: Try my recipe for Grilled Turkey Steak, Wild Rice Pancakes, and Pumpkin Cookies. Believe me, they'll taste completely different in your *sukkah* and they're a creative change from standard holiday fare.

On **Simchas Torah** and **Shemini Atzeres**, it's time to push your culinary daring to the limits. Consider the fact that we've just come through Rosh Hashanah, Yom Kippur, and Sukkos, not to mention a *Shabbos* or two. Everyone at your table is thinking, "If I see one more potato kugel…" So have fun with the menu and try my simple recipes for Stuffed Poblanos (a mild chili pepper) and Mexican Brisket, a fab twist on traditional recipes.

I can't say that **Chanukah** is a dieter's dream holiday, with all of those crisp fried latkes and tantalizing jelly doughnuts. (My exotic Samosa Latkes are worth it!) If you're counting calories, the best advice I can give you is to eat your latkes standing over the sink, because everybody knows that calories consumed over the sink don't count. But take heart; there are no major all-you-can-eat festivals until Purim.

That gives you ten weeks to get Chanukah off your hips, so you can close the zipper on your **Purim** costume. I can't promise you that my Purim recipes will be low-calorie, but they're guaranteed to put you in high spirits (especially my Rum Raisin Bread Pudding!). Just go easy on the spirits, especially if you're the designated driver after the Purim feast.

I'm going to skip over **Passover** in this book, people, not because I don't love it, but because Passover recipes are from a different universe. There's so much to say about Passover cooking—and so many fantastic (and I do mean incredibly yummy) recipes—that I'm saving it all for another book. Please forgive the omission and in the meantime, you have my permission to either raid your Bubbie's recipe box or revisit my first book, *Quick & Kosher:*

*Recipes From The Bride Who Knew Nothing* (with over 40 awesome Kosher for Passover recipes). You can't go wrong with that.

**Shavuos** is one of my favorite food holidays because at heart I'm a dairy lover. While my husband is happy with any holiday meal I cook (as long as it's meat and potatoes), I'd be totally happy with a pasta dish most of the time. Shavuos is my chance to show just how festive and elegant a dairy meal can be. Zero in on my recipe for White Lasagna and watch even your most committed carnivore beg for more.

So take a look at the holiday menus and recipes on the following pages; I know you'll want to try them. Listen, I knocked myself out trying to pair up foods that would work together perfectly for every meal, but if you decide to take one of my Rosh Hashanah recipes and use it on Purim—I'll never know. In fact, for this chapter, I noted the Prep and Total times on each recipe so you can easily create your own menus and still stay within *your* time frame. Go ahead, mix and match to your heart's delight!

{ holiday } meals

# {Roasted Lemon Cornish Game Hens}

Jumbo Potato Pancake | Green Beans with Walnut and Green Olive Tapenade
Sponge Cake with Berry Sauce

**Serves 6**

## Striped Bass Filets

Prep: 5 min. | Total: 20 min.

**Gefen Canola Oil Cooking Spray**
6 **(8-ounce) striped bass filets, with skin**
½ **cup olive oil**
1 **tablespoon kosher salt**
2 **teaspoons freshly ground black pepper**
6 **sprigs fresh rosemary**
6 **slices lemon**

Preheat oven to 425° F. Lightly spray a jelly-roll pan with cooking spray.

Arrange fish on prepared pan. Drizzle oil on fish, and season with salt and pepper. Place 1 sprig rosemary and 1 slice lemon on each filet.

Bake for 12 to 15 minutes, or until fish flakes with a fork.

## Zucchini Soup

Prep: 5 min. | Total: 45 min.

1 **tablespoon canola oil**
1 **medium onion, coarsely chopped**
2 **zucchini, coarsely chopped**
1 **teaspoon fresh thyme**
2 **(32-ounce) boxes Manischewitz Reduced Sodium All Natural Chicken Broth**
1 **teaspoon kosher salt**
½ **teaspoon freshly ground black pepper**
¼ **cup Texmati white rice**

Heat oil in a 4- to 6-quart pot over medium heat. Add onions and cook for 5 minutes. Mix in zucchini and thyme; cook for 5 minutes. Stir in chicken broth, salt, and pepper. Cook for 5 minutes more. Add rice; mix well, and cook for 20 minutes. With an immersion blender or in a food processor, purée until smooth.

## Roasted Lemon Cornish Game Hens

Prep: 10 min. | Total: 1 hr. 10 min.

*Have your butcher split the hens in half for you; it's much easier, and less time consuming, than trying to do it yourself. The vegetables are a "mirepoix," a combination of carrots, celery, and onions, that is used as a base for many dishes, including soups, stews, poultry stuffing, and roasts. Traditionally, when used for roasting, the vegetables are not served but are used rather to infuse flavor into the dish.*

3 **(1 to 1 ½ pounds) Cornish game hens, split in half**
6 **sprigs fresh thyme**
12 **slices lemon**
1 **medium onion, sliced**
1 **carrot, peeled and cut in ½-inch slices**
1 **stalk celery, cut in ½-inch slices**
3 **sprigs parsley**
¼ **cup olive oil**
1 **tablespoon kosher salt**
1 **teaspoon freshly ground black pepper**

*cont. next page*

**Recommended Wine:
Shiloh Chardonnay**

From the striped bass to the game hens with potatoes and the walnut tapenade, this meal calls for a rich white wine. Treat yourself to a full-bodied chardonnay.

Preheat oven to 375° F.

Lift, but don't remove, the skin of the breast of each hen half and place the thyme and 1 or 2 lemon slices between the skin and the meat.

Place the onions, carrots, celery, and parsley in a baking pan large enough to hold the hens.

Place game hens, skin side up, on top of vegetables. Drizzle olive oil over the hens and season with salt and pepper.

Bake for 1 hour. Serve each person one-half a hen.

## Jumbo Potato Pancake

Prep: 10 min. | Total: 55 min.

- 3  **Idaho baking potatoes, scrubbed and dried**
- 1  **teaspoon dried rosemary**
- 2  **teaspoons kosher salt**
- 1  **teaspoon cracked black pepper**
- 1  **egg, lightly beaten**
- 3  **tablespoons pareve margarine, melted and divided**

Preheat oven to 375° F.

Peel potatoes and shred them on the large hole of a grater or in a food processor. Squeeze out excess liquid.

In a large bowl, toss the shredded potatoes with the rosemary, salt, pepper, egg, and 1 tablespoon margarine.

Heat remaining 2 tablespoons margarine in a 6-inch nonstick ovenproof skillet over medium heat. Spread potato mixture over bottom of the skillet to make one large pancake. Cook for 10 minutes. Place in oven and bake for 30 minutes more. Remove from oven and let cool for 5 minutes. Cut into 6 wedges.

## Green Beans with Walnut and Green Olive Tapenade

Prep: 6 min. | Total: 14 min.

*You can use store-bought tapenade to make this dish in even less time. After steaming the green beans, just toss them with the store-bought tapenade and serve.*

- 1  **pound fresh green beans, rinsed, dried, and trimmed**
- 1  **cup halved walnuts**
- ½  **cup pitted green olives**
- ½  **small red onion, coarsely chopped**
- ¼  **cup fresh parsley leaves, coarsely chopped**
- ¼  **cup olive oil**
- 2  **tablespoons white wine vinegar**

In a 3-quart pot fitted with a steamer basket, steam the green beans for 7 minutes until they are bright green and crisp-tender (still should have a little bit of a bite). Using tongs, transfer green beans to a serving bowl.

In a food processor, pulse walnuts, olives, onions, and parsley on and off for about 30 seconds or until desired consistency is reached (should form a paste). Transfer to a small bowl and mix well with olive oil and vinegar. Toss tapenade with green beans and serve.

## Sponge Cake with Berry Sauce

Prep: 5 min. | Total: 30 min.

- 4  **cups assorted frozen unsweetened berries, thawed and drained**
- ¼  **cup sugar**
- 2  **tablespoons chopped fresh mint**
- ¼  **cup fruit liqueur**
- 1  **(1-pound) store-bought sponge or pound cake, sliced in at least 6 slices**
   **Nondairy whipped topping (optional)**

Place berries in a large bowl, sprinkle with sugar, and let sit for 15 minutes. Sprinkle mint on top and pour liqueur over fruit. Stir and let sit for another 10 minutes.

Place a slice of cake on each of six individual dessert plates. Using a slotted spoon, place berries on the cake and top with nondairy whipped topping, if desired.

# {shabbos lunch}

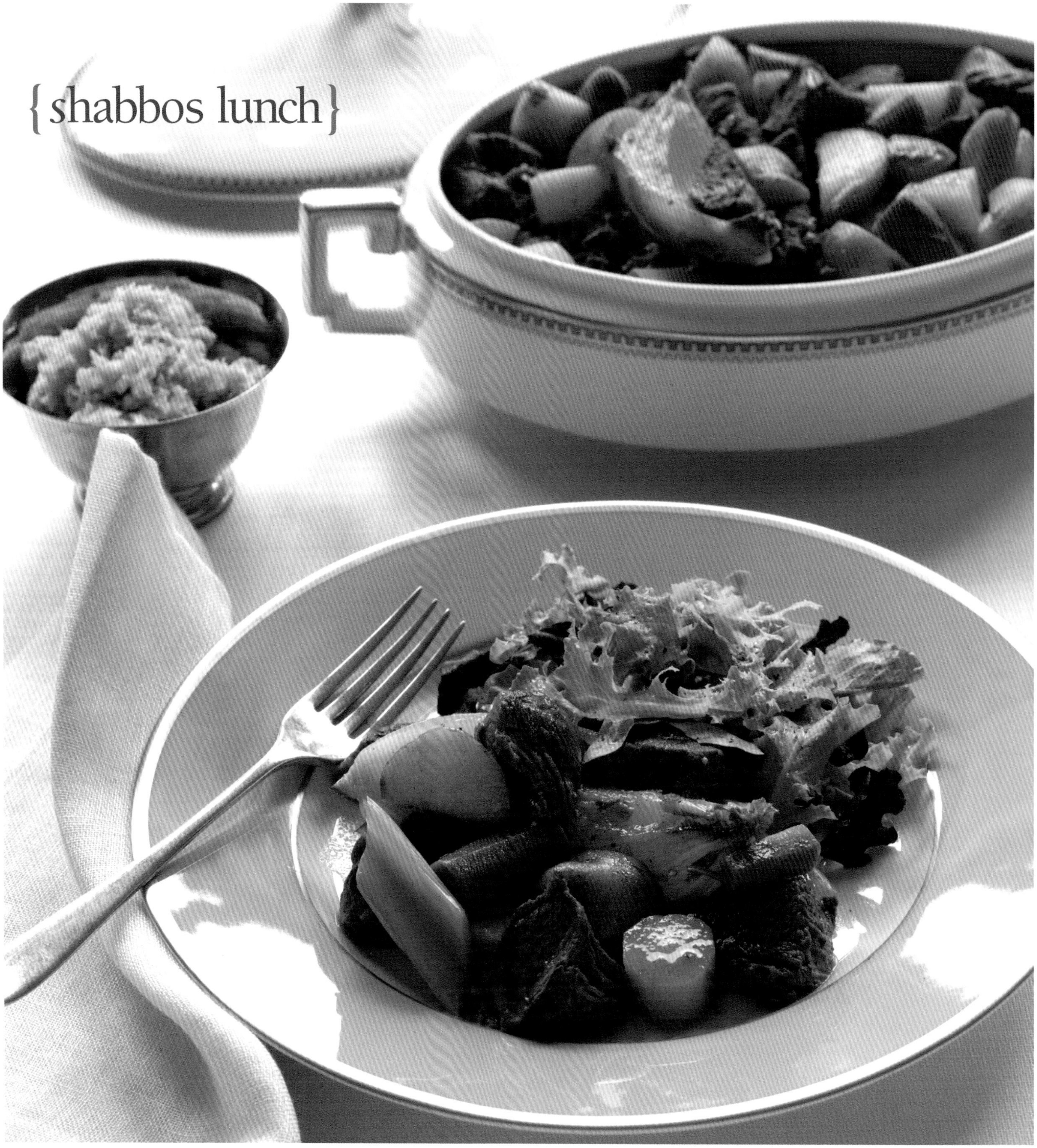

Smoked Trout with Horseradish Mayonnaise

# { Pot au Feu }

House Salad | Green Bean Vinaigrette

Tofutti Ice Cream with Granola and Sliced Peaches

**Serves 6**

## Smoked Trout with Horseradish Mayonnaise

Prep: 5 min. | Total: 10 min.

*This is delicious with a slice of fresh challah.*

¼ cup jarred white horseradish, drained

½ cup **Gefen Regular or Lite Mayonnaise**

2 tablespoons freshly squeezed lemon juice

½ teaspoon cracked black pepper

3 (5-ounce) packages smoked trout, flaked into bite-size pieces

6 lemon wedges

In a small bowl, combine horseradish, mayonnaise, lemon juice, and pepper to make the dressing. Mix well.

In a serving bowl, mix the smoked trout with the dressing and serve with challah. Garnish with lemon wedges.

## Pot au Feu

Prep: 20 min. | Total: 10 hrs. 20 min.

4 large red potatoes, scrubbed and quartered

2 medium onions, quartered

4 garlic cloves, smashed

1 bunch carrots, peeled and cut in 2-inch chunks

3 parsnips, peeled, halved lengthwise, and cut in 2-inch chunks

2 stalks celery, cut in 2-inch chunks

4 pounds beef cubes

3 sprigs fresh flat leaf parsley

2 sprigs fresh thyme

1 bay leaf

1 (32-ounce) box **Manischewitz All Natural Beef Broth**

1 (6-ounce) jar horseradish, any variety

In a slow cooker, layer potatoes, onions, garlic, carrots, parsnips, and celery. Top with the beef cubes, parsley, thyme, and bay leaf. Pour in the beef broth. Cook on low for at least 10 hours. Transfer to a large platter, remove bay leaf and thyme sprigs, and serve with horseradish on the side.

**Recommended Wine:**
**Rothschild Haut Medoc Bordeaux**

This substantial Shabbos meal will hold up nicely to a substantial red wine. Try a good Bordeaux. But be careful, spicy horseradish sauce can be intensified by a tannic red wine.

## House Salad

Prep: 4 min. | Total: 8 min.

- ¼ **cup Bartenura Balsamic Vinegar**
- ½ **cup extra virgin olive oil**
- ½ **teaspoon kosher salt**
- ½ **teaspoon freshly ground black pepper**
- 1 **(5-ounce) package baby salad greens, rinsed and dried**

In a small bowl, whisk together vinegar, olive oil, salt, and pepper. Place greens in a salad bowl. Pour dressing over the greens, toss well, and serve.

## Tofutti Ice Cream with Granola and Sliced Peaches

Prep: 5 min. | Total: 10 min.

- 2 **cups frozen sliced peaches, thawed, or 2 cups fresh peaches, sliced**
- 1 **(64-ounce) container pareve vanilla ice cream**
- 1 **cup granola, any variety**

In each of six dessert bowls, place 2 scoops of ice cream and ⅓ cup peaches. Sprinkle 2 ½ tablespoons granola over top.

## Green Bean Vinaigrette

Prep: 5 min. | Total: 15 min.

*Making this recipe the day before serving allows the flavors to blend and intensify.*

- 1 **pound fresh green beans, rinsed, dried, and trimmed**
- 1 **medium red onion, thinly sliced**
- ⅓ **cup red wine vinegar**
- 1 **tablespoon freshly squeezed lemon juice**
- 1 **tablespoon honey**
- 1 **tablespoon minced shallot**
- ⅔ **cup extra virgin olive oil**
- ½ **teaspoon kosher salt**
- ¼ **teaspoon freshly ground black pepper**

In a 3-quart pot fitted with a steamer basket, steam the green beans for 7 minutes until bright green and crisp-tender (still should have a little bit of a bite). Using tongs, transfer green beans to a serving bowl; add onions and set aside.

Place vinegar, lemon juice, honey, and shallots in a blender or food processor. Pulse to combine. With the blender or processor running, slowly add olive oil. Add salt and pepper. Pour over the beans and onions and toss well.

{*r*osh hashana}

## Leek Soup
# { Chicken with Apples }
## Spinach Salad with Pomegranate Dressing | Roasted Beets
## Carrot Cupcakes

**Serves 4**

### Leek Soup

Prep: 6 min. | Total: 30 min.

*After peeling potatoes, placing them in a bowl and covering them with cold water will keep them from oxidizing. Drain potatoes before using.*

- **2 tablespoons canola oil**
- **1 medium onion, coarsely chopped**
- **2 shallots, coarsely chopped**
- **2 leeks, halved lengthwise, rinsed, and sliced**
- **1 (32-ounce) box Manischewitz All Natural Chicken Broth**
- **2 tablespoons fresh thyme leaves or 2 teaspoons dried**
- **1 large potato, peeled and coarsely chopped**
- **1 teaspoon kosher salt**
- **1 teaspoon freshly ground black pepper**

In a 4- to 6-quart pot, heat oil over medium-high heat. Add onions, shallots, and leeks. Stir, and cook for 5 minutes. Stir in chicken broth and thyme; cover and bring to a boil. Add potatoes, salt, and pepper; mix well and cook for 20 minutes.

Purée soup with an immersion blender or in a food processor. Adjust seasoning, if needed.

........................................

**Recommended Wine:**
**Castel Grand Vin**

A hearty and special *yom tov* meal such as this one which is centered around roasted chicken and beets (the red vegetable that loves a good red wine) calls for a robust cabernet sauvignon-based wine.

### Chicken with Apples

Prep: 10 min. | Total: 1 hr. 5 min.

*Using a mandoline saves a ton of time and will ensure that all ingredients are uniform in size. Not only does it look pretty, but it will also help the apples and vegetables cook evenly.*

- **1 teaspoon ground cinnamon**
- **1 teaspoon mustard powder**
- **1 teaspoon fresh thyme leaves**
- **1 tablespoon kosher salt**
- **1 teaspoon freshly ground black pepper**
- **1 (4-pound) chicken, cut into eighths**
- **1 tablespoon canola oil**
- **1 medium onion, in ¼-inch slices**
- **1 cup sliced fennel, in ¼-inch slices**
- **2 tart apples, unpeeled, cored and in ¼-inch slices**
- **1 cup Manischewitz Reduced Sodium All Natural Chicken Broth**

Preheat oven to 350° F.

In a small bowl, combine the cinnamon, mustard, thyme, salt, and pepper. Rub over the chicken.

Heat oil, over high heat, in an ovenproof sauté pan that is large enough to fit all the chicken in one layer without crowding the pan. If the pan is too small, work in batches. Brown chicken pieces about 4 to 5 minutes on each side. Transfer the chicken to a plate and set aside.

Add onions, fennel, and apples to the sauté pan and cook for 5 minutes, stirring to make sure they don't burn. Return chicken and any accumulated juices to the sauté pan with onions, fennel, and apples; cook for 5 minutes. Add broth and place pan in the oven. Continue cooking for 30 minutes.

Arrange chicken on a large platter. Surround chicken with onions, fennel, and apples. Pour pan juices over top.

## Spinach Salad with Pomegranate Dressing

Prep: 4 min. | Total: 6 min.

- 1 **shallot, minced**
- 2 **tablespoons pomegranate juice**
- 1 **tablespoon Dijon mustard**
- 2 **tablespoons red wine vinegar**
- 1 **teaspoon kosher salt**
- ½ **teaspoon freshly ground black pepper**
- ½ **cup extra virgin olive oil**
- 1 **(5-ounce) package baby spinach, rinsed and dried**
- 1 **cup store-bought croutons**
- ½ **cup pomegranate seeds**

In a small bowl, whisk shallots with pomegranate juice, mustard, vinegar, salt, and pepper. Whisk in olive oil in a steady stream.

In a salad bowl, toss the baby spinach with the croutons and pomegranate seeds. Drizzle with the dressing.

## Roasted Beets

Prep: 5 min. | Total: 1 hr. 5 min.

*To trim and wash beets: Scrub the beets. Leave the skin on and cut off the greens and the root end.*

- 2 **bunches beets (about 3 pounds), scrubbed and trimmed**
- ¼ **cup canola oil**
- 1 **tablespoon kosher salt**
- 1 **teaspoon freshly ground black pepper**

Preheat oven to 400° F. Line a 9- x 13-inch baking pan with foil.

Place beets in prepared pan. Toss beets with oil, salt, and pepper. Add ½ cup water to the pan and cover the pan tightly with foil.

Bake for 45 minutes. Remove beets from oven and allow to cool slightly, about 5 minutes, and peel. Cut into bite-size pieces; adjust seasoning, if needed. Serve at room temperature.

## Carrot Cupcakes

Prep: 15 min. | Total: 40 min. | Yield 20 cupcakes

- 1 **teaspoon baking powder**
- 1 **(2 ½-ounce) jar baby food applesauce**
- 2 **cups flour**
- 1 **cup sugar**
- 2 **teaspoons baking soda**
- 1 ½ **teaspoons ground cinnamon**
- ½ **teaspoon salt**
- ½ **teaspoon vanilla**
- ¼ **cup canola oil**
- 2 **cups grated carrots (about 4 medium carrots), squeezed dry**
- 1 **cup canned drained crushed pineapple**
- ½ **cup confectioners' sugar**

Preheat oven to 350° F. Place 20 paper liners in muffin tins.

In a small bowl, mix the baking powder with the applesauce until it foams. Set aside.

In a large bowl, whisk the flour, sugar, baking soda, cinnamon, and salt together.

Mix in the vanilla, oil, carrots, pineapple, and the applesauce mixture. Mix well until just combined.

Fill lined muffin tins three-quarters full. Bake for 25 minutes.

Remove tins from oven and let cool on a wire rack. Once cupcakes are cool, remove them from the pan. Dust with confectioners' sugar by placing the sugar in a small sieve and shaking the sieve gently over the cupcakes.

{yom kippur}

Italian Wedding Soup
# {Minute Roast with Pan Drippings}
Puréed Parsnips | Braised Carrots with Dill

Chocolate Pretzel Crust Tart

**Serves 6**

## Italian Wedding Soup

Prep: 28 min. | Total: 50 min.

- 1 **tablespoon olive oil**
- 1 **small onion, finely chopped**
- 1 **clove garlic, minced**
- ½ **pound ground beef**
- ¼ **cup finely chopped fresh flat leaf parsley**
- ¼ **cup bread crumbs**
- 1 **large egg, beaten**
- 1 **teaspoon kosher salt**
- ½ **teaspoon freshly ground black pepper**
- ½ **cup ditalini or orzo**
- 2 **(32-ounce) boxes Manischewitz All Natural Chicken Broth**
- ½ **cup frozen spinach, thawed and squeezed dry**

In a small sauté pan over medium-high heat, heat oil and sauté onions for 3 to 4 minutes. Add garlic and cook for 2 minutes more. Let cool slightly.

In a medium bowl, combine onions and garlic with ground beef, parsley, bread crumbs, egg, salt, and pepper. Form into meatballs ½-inch in diameter. Place in freezer for 15 minutes.

While meatballs are chilling, cook pasta according to package instructions.

In a large pot, bring broth to a boil and gently lower meatballs, one at a time into the broth. Reduce heat to simmer and cook, uncovered, for 20 minutes, adding spinach for the last few minutes.

Add pasta. Taste and adjust salt and pepper, if needed.

## Minute Roast with Pan Drippings

Prep: 3 min. | Total: 36 min.

*Using Worcestershire sauce in a meat dish in a kosher kitchen can be tricky because it contains anchovies. Look for a kosher certification mark which is not accompanied by a "fish" notation. That sauce can be used in a meat dish.*

- 1 **(2-pound) minute roast**
- ¼ **cup Montreal Steak Seasoning**
- 2 **tablespoons Worcestershire sauce**
- ½ **cup Manischewitz Reduced Sodium All Natural Chicken Broth**

Preheat oven to 425° F.

Place steak seasoning on a platter; roll the roast in the steak seasoning. Place roast in a small roasting pan and drizzle Worcestershire sauce over the roast.

Insert a meat thermometer into the thickest part of the roast, pushing it in about halfway. Roast for about 30 minutes for medium doneness or until the thermometer reads 160° F. Transfer roast from the pan to a carving board. Remove thermometer and let rest for 5 minutes. Pour beef broth into the hot roasting pan, stirring to get up any bits from the pan.

Slice the roast across the grain and drizzle some of the pan drippings over the meat. Serve remaining drippings in a gravy boat on the side.

**Recommended Wine:
Segal's Cabernet Sauvignon
Special Reserve**

Even though this is a pre-fast meal, it is also a *seudas mitzvah* and can be enjoyed with a glass of wine. The minute roast here will go great with a glass of cabernet sauvignon.

## Puréed Parsnips

Prep: 4 min. | Total: 24 min.

*Choose smaller parsnips, which are younger than the larger ones and don't have woody centers; they will be more tender and sweet.*

1 ½ pounds young parsnips, peeled and cut into
    2-inch lengths
2 tablespoons pareve margarine
1 tablespoon kosher salt

Place parsnips in a medium saucepan with margarine and salt. Cover with water and bring to a boil. Cook for 15 minutes. Reserving ¼ cup cooking liquid, drain the parsnips.

Purée parsnips in a food processor, adding reserved cooking liquid slowly until mixture reaches the desired consistency.

## Braised Carrots with Dill

Prep: 2 min. | Total: 14 min.

1 (16-ounce) bag peeled baby carrots
3 tablespoons pareve margarine, divided
1 ½ teaspoons kosher salt
3 tablespoons finely chopped fresh dill

Place the carrots, 2 tablespoons margarine, and salt in a medium saucepan and cover with water. Bring to a boil. Reduce heat to medium and cook, uncovered, for 12 minutes. Drain carrots and transfer to a serving bowl. Toss with dill and remaining 1 tablespoon margarine.

## Chocolate Pretzel Crust Tart

Prep: 15 min. | Total: 55 min.

*The crust on this recipe calls for salted pretzels. Before Yom Kippur try this with unsalted pretzels so as not to eat anything that will make fasting difficult.*

For pretzel crust:
4 cups whole pretzels
¼ cup sugar
⅓ cup melted pareve margarine

For filling:
2 cups pareve semisweet chocolate chips
2 tablespoons sugar
¼ teaspoon salt
1 ½ cups soy milk
2 large eggs, room temperature
¼ cup roughly chopped salted pretzels
    Nondairy whipped topping

Preheat oven to 350° F.

In a food processor, crush pretzels into fine crumbs.

In a medium bowl, mix pretzel crumbs, sugar, and margarine. Place a 9-inch nonstick tart pan with a removable bottom on a sturdy cookie sheet so it's easier to remove from the oven. Press mixture onto the bottom and up the sides of the pan using a small juice glass to press the mixture down and make the crust even.

Bake for 10 minutes. Remove from oven and let cool completely on a wire rack, about 20 minutes.

Reduce oven to 325° F.

Combine chocolate chips, sugar, and salt, in a medium bowl. In a small saucepan, bring soy milk to a simmer; do not allow to boil. Pour soy milk over chocolate chips and stir until chocolate is melted and smooth, about 2 minutes.

Gently whisk eggs, one at a time, into chocolate mixture. Pour into tart shell and bake for 15 to 20 minutes until filling is set and the surface is glossy. If you see any bubbles or cracks forming on the surface, take the tart out immediately or the filling will be overcooked. Let cool on wire rack for 10 minutes.

Cover with plastic wrap and refrigerate until ready to serve.

Just before serving, top with ¼ cup roughly chopped pretzels.

Serve with nondairy whipped topping.

{ *yom kippur break fast* }

Brie with Infused Honey and Crusty Bread

# {Mediterranean Jack Omelet}

Skillet Potatoes | Three Bean Salad

Poached Pears

. . . . . . . . . . . . . . . . . . . . . . . . . . . . . . . . . . . . . . . . . . . . . . . . . . . . . . . . . . . . . . . . . . . . . . . . . . . . . .

**Serves 6** | This is also a great menu for a special brunch anytime.

## Brie with Infused Honey and Crusty Bread

Prep: 3 min. | Total: 5 min.

*Look for an artisanal honey infused with herbs. You can make your own thyme-infused honey by heating ¼ cup of honey with 3 sprigs of thyme and 1 crushed garlic clove in a small saucepan over low heat for 10 minutes. Remove garlic before serving.*

1  **large French baguette, sliced**

1  **(7-ounce) wheel Les Petites Fermieres Brie**

½  **cup herb-infused honey**

Serve slices of bread with the honey and brie on the side, allowing people to spread and drizzle honey as desired.

## Mediterranean Jack Omelet

Prep: 3 min. | Total: 6 min. | Yield 1 omelet

*Please note that this meal serves six but this recipe serves one. Omelets should be made one at a time. In order to serve six, be sure to have the appropriate amount of ingredients.*

2  **large eggs**

**Pinch kosher salt**

**Pinch freshly ground black pepper**

1  **tablespoon butter**

¼  **cup grated Les Petites Fermieres Mediterranean Jack**

Preheat oven to 200° F. Place dinner plate in oven to warm.

In a medium bowl, beat eggs well; beat in salt and pepper to taste.

Heat butter in an omelet pan or small sauté pan over medium to low heat. Do not let butter brown. Pour eggs into the pan; stir them with the back of a fork over the whole surface of the pan. Once eggs have started to set, about 2 minutes, sprinkle grated cheese over eggs. Let eggs finish cooking without touching them.

When eggs have completely set, remove pan from heat. Gently fold the omelet in half and slide out onto a warmed dinner plate.

. . . . . . . . . . . . . . . . . . . . . . . . . . . . . . . . . . . . . . . . . . . .

**Recommended Wine:**
**Bartenura Moscato**

Though a Break Fast might not be the best time for wine, a light, low-alcohol wine such as a moscato could be just the thing.

## Skillet Potatoes

Prep: 6 min. I Total: 41 min.

 ¼  cup canola oil

 3  Idaho potatoes, peeled and cut in ½-inch cubes

 I  medium onion, coarsely chopped

 I  teaspoon kosher salt

 ½  teaspoon freshly ground black pepper

Over medium-high heat, heat oil in a 12-inch nonstick skillet until shimmering. Sauté potatoes, stirring often until they start to brown, about 25 minutes. Add onions and continue cooking for 10 minutes, stirring for even cooking. Season with salt and pepper.

Remove from pan with a slotted spoon and place on a serving plate. Adjust seasoning, if needed.

## Three Bean Salad

Prep: 7 min. I Total: 38 min.

 I  ½ teaspoons Dijon mustard

 I  ½ teaspoons sugar

 ⅓  cup apple cider vinegar

 ¼  cup olive oil

 ¼  teaspoon kosher salt

   Pinch freshly ground black pepper

 ½  head iceberg lettuce, washed, dried, and torn into bite-size pieces

 I  medium red onion, finely chopped

 I  (14-ounce) can garbanzo beans, rinsed and drained

 I  (14-ounce) can kidney beans, rinsed and drained

 I  (14-ounce) can green beans, rinsed and drained

In a medium bowl, whisk together mustard, sugar, vinegar, oil, salt, and pepper to taste.

In a large salad bowl, combine lettuce, onions, garbanzo beans, kidney beans, and green beans. Toss with dressing. Let sit for ½ hour before serving so the flavors meld.

## Poached Pears

Prep: 10 min. I Total: 45 min.

 4  tablespoons cold butter or pareve margarine, plus more for greasing

 6  Bosc pears

   Juice from 1½ lemons

 ⅔  cup packed brown sugar

 ½  teaspoon ground cinnamon

 ½  cup heavy cream

Preheat oven to 375° F. Grease an 8- x 8-inch square ovenproof baking dish with butter.

Peel pears carefully, making long full strokes with a vegetable peeler so that the pears hold their shape. Halve the pears and use a melon baller to core them. Rub lemon juice all over pears so they do not oxidize.

Fit pears snugly in prepared baking dish.

In a small bowl, using your fingers, combine brown sugar, cinnamon, and margarine until you have pea-sized crumbs. Sprinkle over pears and bake, covered with foil, for 30 minutes.

Using a slotted spoon, transfer pears to a serving plate. Pour cream into the hot baking dish, stirring to get up all the browned bits. Pour sauce over pears and serve.

{sukkos}

Red Leaf Lettuce with Dried Cranberries and Pecans

# { Grilled Turkey Steak }

Wild Rice Pancakes | Broccoli with Lemon Dressing
Pumpkin Cookies

**Serves 6**

## Red Leaf Lettuce with Dried Cranberries and Pecans

Prep: 4 min. | Total: 18 min.

- 1 **cup halved pecans**
- 1 **cup dried cranberries**
- 1 **shallot, minced**
- 1 **tablespoon Dijon mustard**
- ¼ **cup red wine vinegar**
- 1 **teaspoon kosher salt**
- ½ **cup extra virgin olive oil**
- 1 **head red leaf lettuce, washed, dried, and torn into bite-size pieces**
  **Cracked black pepper**

Preheat oven to 350° F.

Spread the pecans on a jelly-roll pan and toast in oven for 10 minutes, stirring often. Keep a close eye on them so they do not burn.

Remove from oven and let cool.

In a small bowl, combine cranberries, shallots, Dijon mustard, vinegar, and salt. Slowly whisk in olive oil.

In a large salad bowl, toss the lettuce with the toasted pecans and drizzle cranberry dressing on top.

## Grilled Turkey Steak

Prep: 2 min. | Total: 30 min.

- **Gefen Canola Oil Cooking Spray**
- 2 **teaspoons kosher salt**
- 1 **teaspoon freshly ground black pepper**
- 1 **teaspoon mustard powder**
- ½ **teaspoon dried thyme leaves**
- ½ **teaspoon dried oregano**
- ¼ **teaspoon dried sage**
  **Pinch ground cloves**
  **Pinch ground allspice**
- 6 **(¼-pound) turkey steaks (from turkey breast)**

Preheat to 350° F. Lightly spray jelly-roll pan with cooking spray.

In a small bowl, whisk the salt, pepper, mustard, thyme, oregano, sage, cloves, and allspice together. Rub onto turkey steaks.

Heat an oiled grill pan over high heat until the pan is smoking. Place turkey steaks on the grill pan and cook for 4 minutes on each side.

Transfer steaks to prepared pan and roast in oven for 20 minutes.

**Recommended Wine:**
**Herzog Reserve Alexander Valley Cabernet Sauvignon**

The turkey steaks and wild rice are prepared in a manner worthy of a red wine, but it should be an elegant wine so as not to overpower the flavors of the meal.

## Wild Rice Pancakes

Prep: 20 min. | Total: 32 min.

*You can warm the maple syrup in the microwave so it doesn't cool off the pancakes when it's poured on top.*

½ **cup potato starch**

1 **teaspoon kosher salt**

¼ **cup soy milk**

1 **large egg, beaten**

2 **cups cooked wild rice**

¼ **cup chopped scallions**

2 **to 3 tablespoons canola oil**

**Maple syrup**

In a large bowl, whisk potato starch and salt with soy milk and beaten egg. Add wild rice and scallions.

Over high heat, heat enough oil to lightly cover the bottom of a large sauté pan; reduce heat to medium. Ladle ¼ cup of batter per pancake into hot oil. Make enough pancakes to fill the pan without overcrowding. For crispy pancakes, make sure the edges don't touch. Cook over medium heat for 2 to 3 minutes on each side. Repeat until all batter is used.

Serve warm with maple syrup.

## Broccoli with Lemon Dressing

Prep: 2 min. | Total: 10 min.

1 **(1-pound) bag frozen broccoli florets**

2 **tablespoons freshly squeezed lemon juice**

½ **teaspoon Gefen Coarse Sea Salt**

½ **teaspoon cracked black pepper**

2 **tablespoons extra virgin olive oil**

Cook broccoli according to package instructions. While the broccoli is cooking, whisk together lemon juice, salt, and pepper in a small bowl. Slowly whisk in the oil. Place broccoli on a serving platter and drizzle dressing over top.

## Pumpkin Cookies

Prep: 10 min. | Total: 35 min. | Yield 24 cookies

1 **cup flour**

2 **teaspoons baking powder**

½ **teaspoon ground cinnamon**

½ **teaspoon ground ginger**

¼ **teaspoon ground allspice**

¼ **teaspoon salt**

¼ **cup pareve margarine**

½ **cup packed light brown sugar**

½ **cup pumpkin purée**

1 **large egg**

Preheat oven to 350° F. Line cookie sheets with parchment paper.

In a medium bowl, whisk together flour, baking powder, cinnamon, ginger, allspice, and salt. Set aside.

In a mixing bowl, with an electric mixer, beat margarine with brown sugar until light and fluffy, 3 to 4 minutes. Beat in pumpkin and egg until well combined. Stir in the dry ingredients and mix well.

Drop by rounded teaspoonfuls 2 inches apart onto prepared cookie sheets.

Bake for 15 minutes. Transfer cookies to a wire rack and let cool completely.

{simchas torah}

Corn Salad
# { Mexican Brisket }
## Stuffed Poblanos | Mexican Pasta
## Banana Chocolate Parfait

. . . . . . . . . . . . . . . . . . . . . . . . . . . . . . . . . . . . . . . . . . . . . . . . . . . . . . . . . . . . . . . . . . . . . .

**Serves 6**

## Corn Salad

Prep: 6 min. | Total: 8 min.

 1  **(11-ounce) can sweet corn niblets, drained**
 1  **small red onion, finely chopped**
 ½  **cup green pepper, seeds and ribs removed, finely chopped**
 ½  **cup red pepper, seeds and ribs removed, finely chopped**
 1 ½ **teaspoons kosher salt**
 ½  **cup finely chopped fresh cilantro**
 ¼  **cup freshly squeezed lime juice**
 1  **tablespoon olive oil**
 6  **leaves Bibb lettuce, rinsed and dried**

In a medium bowl, combine corn, onions, peppers, salt, cilantro, lime juice, and oil.

Place one lettuce leaf on each of six individual plates, evenly distribute salad on top.

## Mexican Brisket

Prep: 5 min. | Total: 1 hr. 25 min.

*Some folks love their brisket just falling apart. After 1 hour and 20 minutes, your brisket will be tender and tasty and slice easily (like for a sandwich). Cook another 2 hours and the meat will just fall apart and melt in your mouth. There are no rules with this one. It's up to you.*

 2  **tablespoons packed dark brown sugar**
 1  **tablespoon kosher salt**
 2  **tablespoons mustard powder**
 1  **tablespoon garlic powder**
 1  **tablespoon ground cumin**
 1  **tablespoon dried coriander**
 1  **teaspoon ancho chili powder**
 1  **(2 ½-pound) beef brisket**
 2  **tablespoons canola oil**
 1  **cup Manischewitz All Natural Beef Broth**

Preheat oven to 375° F.

In a small bowl, whisk together brown sugar, salt, dry mustard, garlic powder, cumin, coriander, and chili powder. Rub the spice mixture all over the meat.

Heat the oil in an ovenproof heavy-bottomed pan such as a Dutch oven. Over high heat, brown brisket for 4 to 5 minutes on each side.

When meat is brown, add broth, cover and place in oven for 1 hour and 20 minutes.

. . . . . . . . . . . . . . . . . . . . . . . . . . . . . . . . . . . . . . .

**Recommended Wine:**
**Ramon Cardova Rioja**

The Mexican theme and brisket main dish are nicely complemented by a fruity Spanish red wine.

## Stuffed Poblanos

Prep: 12 min. | Total: 45 min.

4 large poblano peppers: 3 halved lengthwise,
   1 finely chopped

2 tablespoons canola oil

1 small onion, finely chopped

1 cup peeled and finely chopped butternut squash

1 (14-ounce) can black beans, rinsed and drained

¼ cup fresh cilantro leaves, torn for garnish

Preheat oven to 350° F.

Place the three halved peppers in a baking pan and pour boiling water over them. Cover with plastic wrap and set aside.

Heat the oil in a small sauté pan over medium-high heat. Add onions, the finely chopped pepper, and squash; cook for 5 minutes. Add black beans; stir and remove from heat.

Drain the peppers and fill them with the vegetable stuffing. Place stuffed peppers back in the baking pan. Bake for 20 to 25 minutes.

Serve topped with cilantro.

## Mexican Pasta

Prep: 5 min. | Total: 21 min.

2 tablespoons canola oil

1 small onion, finely chopped

1 clove garlic, minced

½ pound angel hair, broken into quarters

1 (14 ½-ounce) can diced tomatoes, undrained

1 cup Manischewitz All Natural Chicken Broth

¼ cup chopped fresh cilantro stems

½ teaspoon ground cumin

   Kosher salt

   Freshly ground black pepper

Heat oil in large sauté pan over medium heat. Add onions and cook for 5 minutes. Add garlic and pasta; cook, stirring, for about 4 minutes.

Add tomatoes, broth, cilantro stems, and cumin; mix well. Cook for 10 minutes, or until pasta is done. Season with salt and pepper to taste.

## Banana Chocolate Parfait

Prep: 7 min. | Total: 10 min.

1 (3 ¼-ounce) package pareve instant vanilla pudding

2 bananas, thinly sliced diagonally

½ cup dark pareve chocolate, roughly chopped

Prepare pudding according to package instructions.

Set out six parfait dishes or wine glasses. In each dish, layer 2 tablespoons pudding and 5 banana slices; repeat layers. Top with 2 tablespoons pudding and sprinkle with 1 tablespoon chocolate.

{chanukah}

Samosa Latkes

# { Bombay Salmon with Jasmine Rice }

Persian Cucumber Salad

Mango Cardamom Shortcakes with Ginger Whipped Cream

**Serves 6**

## Samosa Latkes

Prep: 15 min. | Total: 40 min.

*Russet potatoes are the best for baking.*

- **3 baking potatoes, peeled and shredded**
- **1 medium onion, finely chopped**
- **½ cup frozen peas, thawed**
- **¼ cup matzoh meal**
- **2 large eggs, beaten**
- **¼ teaspoon curry powder**
- **1 teaspoon kosher salt**
- **1 cup canola oil**
- **Sour cream for serving**
- **1 (10-ounce) jar chutney, any variety**

Line a cookie sheet with paper towels.

In a large bowl, mix together potatoes, onion, peas, matzoh meal, eggs, curry powder, and salt.

In a large nonstick sauté pan, heat ¼ cup oil over high heat until shimmering but not smoking, about 1 minute. Ladle about ¼ cup batter per latke into the hot oil, spreading batter to form a 3-inch round. Make three latkes at a time. Reduce heat to medium and cook for 4 minutes on each side until latkes are golden. Remove from oil and place on paper towels to drain.

Continue making latkes, three at a time, until all of the batter is used. Add oil to the pan as necessary, heating oil after each addition before adding more batter.

Serve with sour cream and chutney.

## Bombay Salmon with Jasmine Rice

Prep: 8 min. | Total: 40 min.

*A salmon steak is cut across the fish to form a slice containing the bones. A filet is taken from the side of the fish, leaving the bones behind.*

- **¼ cup olive oil**
- **6 (10-ounce) salmon steaks**
- **1 teaspoon freshly ground black pepper**
- **1 tablespoon kosher salt, divided**
- **1 tablespoon canola oil**
- **1 medium onion, coarsely chopped**
- **2 cloves garlic, crushed**
- **1 cube frozen crushed ginger**
- **2 teaspoons curry powder**
- **1 teaspoon ground cinnamon**
- **¼ teaspoon ground cardamom**
- **¼ teaspoon turmeric**
- **Pinch ground cloves**
- **1 (14-ounce) can coconut milk**
- **1 cup jasmine rice**

Preheat oven to 475° F. Place a 7- x 9-inch ungreased baking pan in the oven.

*cont. next page*

**Recommended Wine:
Hagafen White Riesling**

The fried latkes and the flavors derived from the medley of spices in the sauce for the salmon steaks require a versatile wine.

## Bombay Salmon with Jasmine Rice, (cont.)

Rub ¼ cup olive oil all over salmon steaks and season with pepper and 2 teaspoons salt. Set aside.

In a medium saucepot, bring 2 cups water and remaining 1 teaspoon salt to a boil over high heat.

In a medium sauté pan, heat 1 tablespoon canola oil over medium heat. Add onions and cook for 5 minutes. Stir in garlic, ginger, curry powder, cinnamon, cardamom, turmeric, and cloves. Mix well and cook for 1 minute more. Slowly stir in coconut milk and bring to a boil. Reduce heat to a simmer and cook for 20 minutes.

Add rice to the boiling water. Reduce heat to a slow simmer. Cover and cook for 20 minutes.

While rice is cooking, remove the baking pan from the oven. Place salmon steaks on the pan and return it to the oven. Immediately reduce heat to 300° F. Bake for 20 minutes or until fish flakes with a fork.

Plate salmon steaks and spoon the sauce over top. Serve with jasmine rice.

## Persian Cucumber Salad

Prep: 4 min. | Total: 10 min.

- **3 Persian cucumbers or 1 English cucumber**
- **⅓ cup red wine vinegar**
- **1 tablespoon honey**
- **1 tablespoon minced shallots**
- **⅔ cup olive oil**
- **½ teaspoon kosher salt**
- **¼ teaspoon freshly ground black pepper**
- **1 small red onion, halved lengthwise and sliced**
- **½ cup golden raisins**

Quarter cucumbers lengthwise and slice them into 2 ½-inch sticks.

Place red wine vinegar, honey, and shallots in blender or food processor. With the blender or processor running, slowly add olive oil. Add salt and pepper.

In a large salad bowl, toss cucumbers, onions, and raisins together. Pour dressing over salad and serve.

## Mango Cardamom Shortcakes with Ginger Whipped Cream

Prep: 10 min. | Total: 55 min.

*Chilling the dough makes it easier to roll out and helps the glutens relax so the dough is not tough. Lining your baking sheet with parchment paper makes clean-up a snap, helps food color more evenly, and prevents food from sticking.*

- **2 cups flour**
- **1 tablespoon sugar**
- **½ teaspoon kosher salt**
- **2 teaspoons baking powder**
- **1 teaspoon ground cardamom**
- **5 tablespoons shortening**
- **⅔ cup whole milk**
- **Flour for kneading**
- **1 cup heavy cream**
- **1 tablespoon confectioners' sugar**
- **¼ teaspoon ground ginger**
- **2 mangoes, pitted, peeled, cut in ½-inch cubes**

Preheat oven to 450° F. Line a jelly-roll pan with parchment paper. In a large bowl, mix flour, sugar, salt, baking powder, and cardamom.

Using a pastry cutter or a fork, cut the shortening into the flour mixture until it resembles coarse meal.

Add the milk and mix together just until combined.

Turn out onto a floured board or work surface. Knead until a dough is formed, about 2 minutes, adding flour as necessary to keep it from being too sticky. Be careful not to knead too much or shortcakes will be tough. Refrigerate for 30 minutes or overnight.

Roll out dough with a rolling pin to ½-inch thickness. Cut into rounds with a 2 ½-inch diameter biscuit cutter or glass.

Place shortcakes on prepared pan and bake for 10 minutes.

Whip heavy cream with confectioners' sugar and ginger until soft peaks form, about 2 minutes.

Transfer shortcakes to a serving platter. Split each shortcake in half horizontally and distribute the mangoes among the shortcakes. Top each with whipped cream.

{*purim*}

Sweet Pea Soup with Mint

# {Baby Lamb Chops with Red Wine Sauce}

Garlic and Chive Mashed Potatoes | Greens with White Wine Vinaigrette
Rum Raisin Bread Pudding

Serves 6

## Sweet Pea Soup with Mint

Prep: 4 min. | Total: 40 min.

*To quickly thaw peas, cover them with cold water and drain when ready to use.*

- 1 tablespoon olive oil
- 1 medium onion, coarsely chopped
- 1 (32-ounce) box Manischewitz Reduced Sodium All Natural Chicken Broth
- 1 teaspoon kosher salt
- ½ teaspoon freshly ground black pepper
- 1 (1-pound) package frozen peas, thawed
- ¼ cup finely chopped fresh mint

Heat oil in a medium saucepan over medium heat and cook onions for 5 minutes. Stir in chicken broth, salt, and pepper. Cook for 20 minutes, uncovered. Add peas and cook for 5 minutes.

In a food processor or with an immersion blender, purée the soup until smooth, about 5 minutes. Adjust seasoning, if needed.

Ladle soup into bowls and garnish with mint.

## Baby Lamb Chops with Red Wine Sauce

Prep: 5 min. | Total: 20 min.

- 12 baby lamb chops (about 5 pounds)
- 2 tablespoons kosher salt
- 2 teaspoons freshly ground black pepper
- 4 tablespoons canola oil, divided
- ½ cup minced shallots
- 1 cup recommended red wine (see below)
- 1 cup Manischewitz All Natural Beef Broth

Preheat oven to 200° F.

Season chops with salt and pepper.

Over high heat, heat 2 tablespoons oil in each of two large sauté pans. Place chops in one layer in each pan. If all the chops will not fit at one time, brown them in two batches. Cook chops until brown, about 3 minutes on each side. When chops are cooked to your desired doneness, remove from pan and place on a baking sheet. Cover tightly with foil. Place in oven and turn oven off. Chops will stay warm in the retained heat without overcooking.

Reserving 2 tablespoons fat, drain fat from the pans. Return the reserved fat to one sauté pan, over medium heat. Add shallots and cook, stirring, for 1 minute. Add red wine and broth and cook until sauce is reduced by half, about 4 minutes.

Serve lamb chops topped with sauce.

**Recommended Wine:**
**Herzog Special Reserve Edna Valley Syrah**

The gamey flavors in baby lamb chops, especially those prepared with a red wine sauce, make a natural pairing with Old-World-style Syrah.

## Garlic and Chive Mashed Potatoes

Prep: 10 min. | Total: 35 min.

- 6 medium Yukon gold potatoes, peeled and quartered
- 2 cloves garlic
  Kosher salt
- 1 cup Manischewitz All Natural Chicken Broth
- 4 tablespoons pareve margarine
- 2 tablespoons chopped chives

Place potatoes and garlic in a large saucepan and cover with salted water. Bring to a boil and boil gently for 20 minutes or until the potatoes are tender and break apart with a fork. Drain potatoes and return them to the pan.

Heat broth for 30 seconds in the microwave. Heat margarine in the microwave for 20 seconds.

With a potato masher or hand mixer, mash potatoes and garlic with broth, margarine, chives, and salt to taste. Mash potatoes to desired consistency.

## Greens with White Wine Vinaigrette

Prep: 5 min. | Total: 9 min.

- ⅓ cup white wine vinegar
- 1 tablespoon honey
- 1 tablespoon minced shallot or onion
- ⅔ cup olive oil
- ½ teaspoon kosher salt
- ¼ teaspoon freshly ground black pepper
- 1 (5-ounce) package mixed baby greens, rinsed and dried

Place vinegar, honey, and shallots in a blender or food processor.

With the blender or processor running, slowly add olive oil. Blend in salt and pepper.

In a large salad bowl, toss the greens with the dressing and serve.

## Rum Raisin Bread Pudding

Prep: 10 min. | Total: 40 min.

*Don't have day-old bread? Place bread cubes on a baking sheet in the oven at 350° F for 5 minutes to dry out.*

- 1 tablespoon pareve margarine
- 6 cups cubed day-old bread
- 3 cups soy milk
- 2 large eggs
- 1 cup packed light brown sugar
- 2 tablespoons rum
- 1 teaspoon vanilla
- 1 teaspoon ground cinnamon
  Pinch ground nutmeg
- ½ cup raisins
  Nondairy whipped topping

Preheat oven to 350° F. Grease a 9-inch square baking dish with margarine.

Place bread cubes in a large bowl.

In a medium bowl, beat soy milk, eggs, brown sugar, rum, vanilla, cinnamon, nutmeg, and raisins. Pour over the bread and mix thoroughly.

Spoon bread mixture into the prepared baking dish. Let rest for 20 minutes.

Bake for 30 minutes or until a knife inserted in the center comes out clean.

Serve warm with whipped topping on the side.

{shavuos}

# Mini Caprese Salad
# { White Lasagna }
### Broccoli Rabe with Balsamic Vinaigrette | Creamy Caesar Salad
### Strawberry Pastry Cups

**Serves 8**

## Mini Caprese Salad

Prep: 3 min. | Total: 5 min.

- **2 pints grape tomatoes, rinsed and dried**
- **1 (1-pound) container Natural & Kosher Marinated Ciliegine (fresh mozzarella balls)**
- **18 basil leaves, rolled up and sliced into thin strips**
- **½ cup extra virgin olive oil**
- **¼ cup red wine vinegar**
- **Cracked black pepper**

Combine tomatoes, mozzarella balls, and basil in a medium bowl.

Drizzle olive oil and vinegar over the salad and season to taste with cracked black pepper.

**Recommended Wine:**
**Hagafen Oak Knoll Chardonnay**

Cheese and cream are themes in this traditional *milchig* Shavuos meal. Try an oaked California chardonnay whose creaminess will enhance the flavors of the meal.

## White Lasagna

Prep: 15 min. | Total: 1 hr. 40 min.

- **Gefen Canola Oil Cooking Spray**
- **1 (1-pound) box lasagna noodles**

For white sauce:
- **2 tablespoons flour**
- **½ teaspoon mustard powder**
- **Pinch ground nutmeg**
- **2 tablespoons butter**
- **3 cups whole milk**
- **Kosher salt**
- **Freshly ground black pepper**

For filling:
- **1 (10-ounce) package frozen spinach, thawed and squeezed dry**
- **2 cups Natural & Kosher Ricotta Cheese**
- **1 cup Natural & Kosher Grated Parmesan**
- **1 large egg, beaten**
- **Kosher salt**
- **Freshly ground black pepper**

For assembly:
- **1 cup Natural & Kosher Grated Parmesan**
- **1 cup Natural & Kosher Shredded Mozzarella**

Preheat oven to 375° F. Lightly spray a deep-dish lasagna pan with cooking spray.

Cook lasagna noodles according to package instructions. Drain, rinse under cold water. Drain again and set aside.

To make white sauce: In a small bowl, whisk flour with mustard and nutmeg.

In a medium saucepan, heat butter over medium heat. Whisk in flour mixture. Continue cooking over medium heat until the butter and flour start to bubble (it will look like honeycombs), about 1 to 2 minutes.

*cont. next page*

## White Lasagna, (cont.)

Heat milk in microwave for 45 seconds. Very slowly whisk heated milk into the saucepan. Reduce heat to medium and cook, stirring often, for 15 to 20 minutes or until thickened. Season with salt and pepper to taste.

To make filling: In a large bowl, combine spinach, ricotta cheese, Parmesan, egg, and salt and pepper to taste.

To assemble: Spread one-quarter of the white sauce on the bottom of the pan. Top with a single layer of noodles then one-third of ricotta filling. Repeat layers twice. Spread remaining sauce on top and sprinkle with Parmesan and mozzarella.

Bake for 45 minutes. Serve warm right out of the baking dish.

## Broccoli Rabe with Balsamic Vinaigrette

Prep: 5 min. I Total: 15 min.

*If there is any water clinging to the broccoli rabe when you put it in the oil, the oil will splatter and you can get burned; so be sure to dry it very well.*

2 bunches broccoli rabe, rinsed and dried
¼ cup olive oil
4 cloves garlic, minced
½ cup Manischewitz All Natural Vegetable Broth
2 tablespoons Bartenura Balsamic Vinegar
   Kosher salt
   Freshly ground black pepper

Trim the ends of the broccoli rabe and slice into 2-inch pieces. Rinse under cold water. Drain and pat dry with paper towels.

Heat olive oil in large sauté pan and cook garlic for about 1 minute. Add broccoli rabe. When it has wilted a bit, about 4 minutes, add broth. Mix well and continue cooking for 5 minutes. Add vinegar and stir. Transfer to a serving platter. Season with salt and pepper to taste, and serve.

## Creamy Caesar Salad

Prep: 5 min. I Total: 10 min.

1 cup Gefen Regular or Lite Mayonnaise
2 tablespoons freshly squeezed lemon juice
1 tablespoon Worcestershire sauce
2 cloves garlic, minced
1 teaspoon smashed anchovies or anchovy paste
2 tablespoons whole milk
1 head romaine lettuce, rinsed and dried, torn into bite-size pieces
1 cup Natural & Kosher Shredded Parmesan

In a medium bowl, whisk together, mayonnaise, lemon juice, Worcestershire sauce, garlic, anchovies, and milk.

Place greens and cheese in a salad bowl. Toss with dressing to taste. Serve remaining dressing on the side.

## Strawberry Pastry Cups

Prep: 5 min. I Total: 10 min.

4 ounces cream cheese
2 cups store-bought vanilla pudding
16 mini pastry shells
6 strawberries, hulled and sliced

Beat cream cheese with an electric mixer until soft and fluffy, about 2 minutes. Beat in vanilla pudding for about 1 minute.

Spoon filling into pastry shells. Garnish with sliced strawberries.

# {Spotlight} WHAT'S NEW IN KOSHER

By now, you've noticed that I'm partial to certain companies that manufacture

or market foods that are my faves. And, if you know anything about me,

you know that I'm not content until I meet the people behind those products.

I love to explore what motivated them and ask them for consumer tips in their

particular area of food expertise. Since you and I are old friends now, I want

to share with you what they told me. Read on …

# { Become an Expert Wine Taster in 10 Minutes Flat }

Many people are convinced that wine connoisseurs are an elite group of sophisticated Frenchmen who judge wines according to esoteric criteria totally incomprehensible to the rest of us. "Not true," says Jay Buchsbaum, Director of Wine Education at Royal Wine.

When I called Jay for this interview, I asked if he could work his magic and turn me into a wine savant quickly and painlessly. I'm happy to report that he took on the challenge! Here's our quickie crash course.

**Q:** Jay, when you talk about wine tasting, you always mention the "Five S's." What are they and why do they matter?
**A:** Sight, swirl, smell, savor, and spit (or swallow).

**Q:** It's Ok to spit? (Don't tell my kids!)
**A:** At a wine judging, it's expected; but at your dining room table, you can swallow instead. We'll get to that.

**Q:** Let's start with Sight. What are we looking for?
**A:** Color and clarity. In white wines, you should look for color that can go from almost clear to a kind of golden brown. Red wines go from almost purple to brick brown. You want something in between. By the way, all color comes only from the skins of the grapes. The juice is always clear. Clarity means that it shouldn't have stuff floating in it or have a milky look.

**Q:** I've noticed that frequently you do see sediment at the bottom of the bottle. Does that mean the wine is bad? Should you throw it out?
**A:** Great question. If you see sediment, let the wine stand for an hour in an upright position, so when you pour it, the sediment will be in the bottom of the bottle and not float in the wine.

**Q:** So it doesn't mean that the wine is bad.
**A:** No, but if it's in your glass, it's a problem.

**Q:** The next "S" is Swirl. What does that mean?
**A:** Do this and you'll look like a connoisseur! You put the stemmed glass on the table and move it in a circular motion: This will allow the wine to flatten up against the side of the glass and exposes more of its surface to the air. It's like when you open a can of your favorite coffee: You pull the vacuum seal off, hear that whoosh when the air hits it, and then wow! That aroma hits you. The more you expose your wine to the air, the more aroma can be released.

**Q:** And are wine aromas as strong as coffee? Does it come right at you or is it more subtle?

**A:** With coffee, you get that aroma when you first open it, but when you perk it, that's when the aroma really fills the room. It's the same with wine. When you first pour it into the glass, you get that first pop of aroma, but as more of it is exposed to the air, flattened out by swirling it, a more intense aroma hits your senses. However, some wines lose their aromatics quickly, so you should look out for that. And yes, you do have to stick your nose into the glass to experience it. The more you use your sense of smell, the more flavors you will taste.

**Q:** What are we looking for in the aroma?

**A:** Something pleasant, something you can identify. Does it smell like chocolate or fruit, or does it smell like alcohol? You're looking for the confluence of aromas that come together in a pleasant fashion, and also that you can identify individually as well.

**Q:** Do you need a fabulously trained nose to be able to tell the difference?

**A:** It's enough for it to just smell good. But people ask me, "How can you tell the difference between a cabernet and a chardonnay?" I respond, "Can you tell the difference between Coke and store brand cola?" It's the same with wine. Experience teaches you to discern nuances.

**Q:** The next "S" is Savor—please explain.

**A:** As a chef, you know that the tongue has different parts that taste different sensations...

**Q:** Oh Jay, I'm not really a chef…

A: You cook like a chef.

**Q:** I dabble…

**A:** Quite successfully, it seems. Anyway—when you put wine in your mouth, gargle it around so your tongue senses it on all sides: The tip gets the sweetness, the sides get the bitterness or acidity, the back gets the dryness and the middle gets the fullness—so you get all the different aspects of the taste.

**Q:** Uh oh. Are you doing something wrong if you just swallow it?

**A:** For wine tasting purposes, yes, you are. I taste wines frequently, so it's second nature for me to savor it for a while on my tongue. You don't want to be obvious about it at a dinner party. But if you are doing an actual wine tasting, it's perfectly polite to hold it in your mouth for awhile.

**Q:** What about that last "S"—Spit?

**A:** Most people think that's the end. But after you spit or swallow the wine, take a moment and see how long the flavor continues to linger—that's called the finish. The longest finishes are two or three minutes, max. Also, notice what kind of taste it leaves. Is it bitter? Pleasant? Does it change? First, it may be acidic and then you taste a sweetness coming in.

**Q:** Are these judgments objective? Is the wine good or bad and not subject to my experience?

**A:** It's subjective to some degree. People like different things. As people grow in their taste for wine, they go drier and drier and they can taste more nuances.

# BARTENURA

— PRODUCT OF ITALY —

Product of Italy / Produit d'Italie

2 0 0 9

PROVINCIA DI PAVIA
INDICAZIONE GEOGRAFICA TIPICA

## MOSCATO

5% alc./vol.                    750 mL

**Q:** So when you like dry wines, have you arrived as a connoisseur?

**A:** Actually, they say in our business that the novice starts out with sweet wines, then dry whites, then dry reds, then ends up back at sweet wines in the form of dessert wines—French sauternes, Hungarian tokays, ports. Those sweet wines have not only lingering, luscious sweetness to them, they also have such different nuances of aromas and tastes—they're just wonderful!

**Q:** Do we have to be doing nothing else when we drink wine? Should we be concentrating entirely on the wine?

**A:** Initially, when you are learning about wine, yes. But don't get too caught up in it. Just enjoy the wine and think a little about what you are drinking. A nice idea is to have a few couples over for dinner and a wine tasting. (If there are a few people, nobody drinks too much.)

**Q:** Can't do that in hurry. When you're rushing your kids into their pajamas—that's not a good time to experience a new wine, right?

**A:** In that scenario, you gulp the wine down first—then you can deal with the kids.

**Q:** So, the children are tucked into bed, our friends have come over for dinner and a wine tasting. Sounds dreamy.

**A:** You owe this to yourself once in a while. At the beginning of each course, take a moment to sip a new wine, do the Five "S's," then go on with the meal. After a few times, you'll automatically become an expert.

**Q:** So how do I start?

**A:** First of all, don't take it too seriously. Ask a local retailer whom you trust. Tell him what you like and what you're serving for dinner, and let him suggest a wine or two for you to try. Enjoy; chill out. In time, you'll learn to love it.

**Q:** I'm chilling… just want to know, am I taking out a second mortgage to pay for this wine tasting soiree?

**A:** Relax. Don't splurge on an expensive wine if your palate is not educated to appreciate the difference. You can get a good bottle without spending a fortune. As a general rule of thumb, stick with brands that are known for their consistent quality and good value, especially if you're a novice. If you walk in the store and you don't recognize the name, it may be great—but it could be terrible. But a name brand has to make sure that they are always good so consumers will keep coming back.

**Q:** Can you name a few?

**A:** Baron Herzog, Barkan, Bartenura, Binyamina, Castel, Teal Lake, Goose Bay… and there are others, of course.

**Q:** Ok – I'm ready to make up my guest list for the Grand Geller Wine and Dine! Jay, will you come?

**A:** Sure. Um, maybe you should let me bring the wine…

**Jay and I have wine tasting videos online! Watch and learn at blog.Kosher.com**

# { Kosher.com: It's *All* About the Food }

Personally, when I entertain, and put that brisket on the table, I need to know it's gonna be a winner (after all… I've got a "rep to protect"). A great recipe is important, people, but no recipe in the world can help you if your ingredients are subpar. For me, it all begins with the quality of the food. Start with a fresh piece of meat, produce in season and best-in-class brands and you're well on your way to culinary stardom, no matter who you are. (If you need a little more of a tutorial you can check out my cooking videos at blog.Kosher.com.)

Kosher.com is known for its quality, selection and price, and shopping for food online is a trend that's growing faster with every mouse click. And I'm part of it! Folks, I want you to meet Henry Kauftheil, Chairman of Kosher.com, the man who brought me into the "world's largest online kosher supermarket" and gave me my wings!

**Q:** We all know people are shopping for books, cameras, even soulmates online—seems only natural that kosher food should follow.
**A:** It's a no-brainer. Today, it's all about shopping from the comforts of home, without ever leaving your couch or cup of coffee behind.

**Q:** I always tell people we treat a *babka* like a baby. I got that line from you!
**A:** It's the truth: We handle the food with as much care as you would. Our customers know that their goods will arrive intact, just as they left our warehouse shelves, perfectly packaged and delivered on time!

**Q:** What impact do you see online shopping having on the kosher community?
**A:** Though it may sound dramatic, I can honestly say it has revolutionized kosher shopping in at least two ways. You have the shopper who lives near a kosher supermarket, who may normally spend several hours every week pushing around a heavy shopping cart. Now everything can be ordered in just minutes and the time saved is invaluable!

**Q:** It's like my book: I say, cook *'Quick & Kosher'* so you'll have time to do all the other things you love. Kosher.com offers the same advantage.
**A:** Exactly. The second important change is that people who do not live in or near a large Jewish community can have the same selection of kosher foods available instantly. They can even order prepared foods not often found in outlying areas.

**Q:** So was your original vision a two-fold goal? Convenience and access to products not found locally?

**A:** There's always been just one goal: Make the customers' lives easier wherever they may be. Give them access to a premium butcher, fresh-baked goods, prepared foods by well-known kosher leaders like Chap-a-Nosh, Schwartz Appetizing, Simply Sushi, fresh fish from Ossie's, in addition to hard-to-find items and all the regular things you would find in your grocery store.

**Q:** With 15,000 products, I'd say we've got all bases covered.

**A:** That's the idea. One stop. But our most popular departments both locally and nationally, are meat and bakery. Listen, even if you have a good local bakery—who can resist Zomick's challah, rugelach, and cheese-cakes? And we have so many varieties of each: Whole wheat, chocolate chip, and even a super "Simcha Challah" that can feed 50 people. Then there are rugelach in chocolate, vanilla, and cinnamon, heimish and flaky varieties, even dairy…

**Q:** The dairy rugelach are to die for!

**A:** Hey, don't interrupt me when I am on a roll—danishes and chocolate horns, bow ties and cinnamon sticks…

**Q:** You don't have to list everything, Henry. People can just visit us online. But I would be remiss if I didn't mention the fresh cupcakes. They're the absolute best treat I can bring home from Kosher.com. They don't last long in my house, and I can't even blame Hubby or the kids. I just can't walk past those cupcakes without caving in and ruining my diet.

**A:** I'm sure the people at Zomick's will be glad to hear it.

**Q:** Well, there's also Butterflake Bakery's nut-free cinnamon raisin challah: Now that's a "one-bite-and-feel-like-you're-in-heaven" experience too.

**A:** I thought you were partial to our fresh meat selection.

**Q:** That's when I cook, not snack, Henry. But you're right: In cooking, it's all about quality ingredients. I don't have to tell you that having a selection of superb, fresh meats at Kosher.com makes all the difference. When meat is the star of my meal, I want that dish to shine brightly!

**A:** And you don't necessarily have to spend a lot to get the best quality meat. I always tell people to shop our circular.

**Q:** Our specials are practically free.

**A:** Now you're exaggerating.

**Q:** I've been called dramatic more than once in my life. But come on, the prices are so competitive, it's hard to find a better blow-out sale. Henry, where do you think is the furthest we've shipped kosher food?

**A:** Well, we've shipped to U.S. soldiers in Iraq and to schools in Ukraine—not places where kosher food is abundant.

**Q:** Yet so much of our business is from New York City and surrounding areas—places where people *can* get kosher food—but they choose to shop at Kosher.com because it's so easy and so good!

**A:** Those are the stats, thank G-d. They speak for themselves.

**Q:** One reason I prefer shopping online is because it eliminates the stress of picking the perfect melon. Now that we have Kosher.com I don't know why anyone would voluntarily sign up for the pressure of picking produce. It's so great to have someone do that for you.

**A:** We do that and so much more. I tell people, just say the word—online, fax, or phone—and we'll be there with your melons or whatever else you need. And don't worry about freshness. We have a proprietary system for picking, packing, and shipping food anywhere in the U.S.—so it arrives fresh. And to many parts in the NY, NJ, and CT region, we offer free next-day delivery by refrigerated truck. Your order is picked fresh just moments before our truck leaves for your house, with fresh bakery and meat cut to order.

**Q:** Now you're getting serious about this.

**A:** I figured I'd leave talking about the fun stuff to you.

**Q:** If I've done my job right, all of my readers are aware that we have cooking videos, thousands of recipes—even some new and unpublished *Quick & Kosher* recipes developed especially for Kosher.com— and my blog, of course!

**A:** Don't forget the urls: www.Kosher.com and blog.Kosher.com

**Q:** That's why you're the business guy.

**A:** There's one more very important point: At Kosher.com, you can shop with confidence, knowing that we are under strict kosher supervision and a reliable *hashgacha*. We want you to have total peace of mind. That's the whole idea.

**Q:** Henry, I think we should change our name to "kosher-dot-calm."

**A:** Let me sleep on it.

# { Cheese That's Simply "Magnifique!" }

At last, a kosher cheese company that satisfies family needs and gourmet tastes. A daring and resourceful French Jewish woman named Brigitte Mizrahi is the founder of Anderson International Foods, Inc. As a mother, she wanted to supply family-friendly cheeses that are high quality and healthy for our children. And as a gourmet, she felt impelled to bring a line of specialty cheeses to the kosher market. Brigitte met with success and her cheeses now enjoy well-deserved popularity all over the U.S. It was a tough climb, but as Brigitte herself says, "Throw me in the water and I'll figure out how to swim!" Here is my interview with this entrepreneur extraordinaire!

**Q:** How did the idea for this company come about?

**A:** My background is really banking—I have an MBA from NYU. I was always passionate about business. To make a long story short, I left banking after 12 years and started looking for something else to do. I love ceramics—and at first, I wanted to import decorative plates to the U.S. from Tunisia. But the Tunisian economic attaché said to me, "Right now we need someone to import olive oil!" I thought—why not? I can go from ceramics to olive oil.

While the oil was making its way across the ocean by boat, a customer of my distribution partner came into the office and said he wanted to sell his kosher cheese business. So, while waiting for the olive oil to arrive, I went "into" cheese!

I knew nothing about it, but I found a seminar in California and slowly learned all about cheese production. Working with the Rabbis at "Ⓚ Kosher Certification," I learned about *Chalav Yisrael* and *Chalav Stam*, which are different levels of rabbinic milk supervision.

I always go for the best, so I approached the biggest, best quality-controlled plant in the state, Golden Cheese of California. I said, "I want to make kosher cheese," explained what "kosher" means, and I was really fortunate that they went for the idea. They helped me set up a kosher division there. That was about 13 years ago.

**Q:** I'm surprised that that you started this company yourself, because if anyone would have asked me, I would have said, "She's French, she's fabulous, and her family has been making cheese for hundreds of years." So which was the first *Chalav Stam* cheese you put on the market?

**A:** It was our Les Petites Fermieres line. That's "little farm girls" in French. I came across a picture of two little girls from Brittany. They reminded me of my own two daughters, so the picture really spoke to me. I knew this would be the perfect image for our logo. It was my way of saying, "I'm French!" After all, there is something French about producing quality cheeses.

**Q:** What is your family history? Did it play a role in your enterprise?

**A:** We're Sephardic Jews and my parents came from Egypt. My grandfather was in the spice business, and like all Jewish families, we were into food. My mom had a French restaurant. So I grew up surrounded by delicious food.

**Q:** So good food is in your bones.

**A:** My parents bought the best cheeses and we always had wine on the table. We would go on picnics and have Camembert sandwiches.

**Q:** When did you start distributing Les Petites Fermieres?

**A:** October 1997. You may not have heard of it till now because it takes time and persistence to break into the market.

**Q:** It may have taken a while, but you certainly have arrived—in a big way. How does it feel?

**A:** When you're a small business, you think you're like a small tree: A little bit of wind and you're going to break. Now I feel stronger, but I don't ever want to lose that sense of modesty, because in business you never fully arrive. There's always something you can do better. Right now, it's nice not to fight for survival, but to grow. I'm blessed with the most incredible colleagues, and our teamwork is a crucial factor. We all feel that we have a message we want to share with the community.

**Q:** What is your message?

**A:** We have really great cheeses that go with today's lifestyle! There's a whole new generation of people like me. I love having friends over and serving terrific food, but I'm always busy and I don't have much time to cook.

**Q:** Now you're speaking my language! What's your favorite easy dish for entertaining?

**A:** I broil salmon topped with French grainy mustard and serve it with a salad of fresh mozzarella, tomatoes, and basil. Another variation is to broil salmon covered in pesto sauce and serve it with a side salad made from cherry or grape tomatoes and bite-size mozzarella balls.

Muenster

GREAT FOR SNACK

PASSOVER YEAR ROUND

KOSHER
Ⓚ

CHOLOV YISROEL KOSHERED AT 212°

RENNET FREE

rBST FREE

*No significant difference has been shown between milk derived from rBST-treated and non-rBST-treated cows.

Net Wt. 6oz (170g)

**Q:** When I shop, I look at packaging—and I love the look of yours. Recently, while my husband was placing our regular Kosher.com order, he bought your Natural & Kosher American slices for our kids' lunches, and he called out, "Look at this! I got that cheese you love, and at a great price!" So you met two needs—I look for great quality and packaging, and he looks at price. You satisfied us both!

**A:** It's your eyes that do the shopping first, so for me the packaging had to be the best it could be. We came up with the idea of icons to simplify shopping choices.

**Q:** YES! Those icons tell me that I'm making a healthy choice for my family. Can you explain what these symbols mean?

**A:** RBST free = hormone free. We were one of the few companies 10 years ago that chose to use milk from cows not injected with hormones. All our cheeses are natural and we see to it that the milk comes from farms where there is good treatment of the animals. That's represented by another icon. We also have an organic icon and a "0 transfat" symbol. Of course, as a kosher cheese, there's no animal-based rennet—which is important to vegetarians.

**Q:** What varieties do you offer?

**A:** We have 3 labels:
- Natural & Kosher (*Chalav Yisrael*)
- Les Petites Fermieres (*Chalav Stam*) and
- Organic & Kosher (*Chalav Stam*)

We started that last one this past year; I saw there was a need for a line of good organic cheese in the kosher community.

**Q:** Why is it important to you to produce the specialty cheeses?

**A:** Because you can't have fun with just mozzarella! We found a French guy in Canada who was willing to make kosher Brie. As a gourmet company, we're always looking for different flavors. I especially love our Mediterranean Jack: It has great flavoring—sun-dried tomatoes, peppers, and olives. You can make a fabulous omelet with it—an omelet with a kick!

Camembert is soft, similar to Brie. Creamy and luscious, it's fun to melt it, or you can just eat it on a cracker. There are all those amazing, flavor-infused honeys on the market too. I put a little honey or jam on top—and it's amazing.

**Q:** Any tips on serving cheese that we might not know?

**A:** With all cheeses, it's best to let them air outside the refrigerator for about an hour before eating to bring out the flavor. But I just can't wait sometimes, so I eat our yummy Brie straight from the fridge.

**Q:** Straight from the fridge—that's my style too. Brigitte, you've made it possible for kosher families to eat delicious, nourishing meals that are quick to prepare and easy on the budget. And the fact that you take such care to keep your products natural and healthy gives us true peace of mind. Thank you!

**A:** Bon appétit!

# { They Read My Mind! }

Like an explorer searching for the Northwest Passage, I've been looking for a truly delish heat and eat soup. So when I discovered the new Manischewitz ready-to-serve broths, I felt like someone had heard my prayers! Curious Jamie wanted to know how a mass-produced broth could actually taste like it came right out of that old red-rimmed porcelain pot in Grandma's kitchen. So I called up Manischewitz and asked. Below is my enlightening discussion with David Yale, President and CEO of The Manischewitz Company.

**Q:** I love all of your new broths, but I get the most mileage out of the chicken flavored one. Did these soups take long to develop?
**A:** It was a two-year process. We knew what kind of taste we were after, but it took a while to perfect it. Once we had created a sample, we considered top quality in our own kitchen, we took it to outside testing companies to try out on consumers.

**Q:** Ok, I won't mince words any more. How did you get my grandmother's chicken soup recipe?
**A:** It's not your grandmother's recipe.

**Q:** Yes it is.
A: She wouldn't give it to us, Jamie. Listen, we all have warm recollections of our grandma's best cooking. Manischewitz set out to duplicate that taste and aroma. And we did it by making the broth the same way you —or your grandmother—would at home. We cook our broths using only natural ingredients, and in small batches, not like large companies that produce in a high-speed facility.

**Q:** Ah, small batches. That's the secret.
**A:** I guess you could say so. And it certainly works best for our broths. When consumers tasted them "blind" (without knowing what brand it is), they overwhelmingly chose Manischewitz over the other leading national brands.

**Q:** So here's *my* little secret: I use soup stock as a starter in most of the dishes I cook, except for desserts. And I really want it to taste like my grandmother's did—only I don't have the time to dice and slice and simmer all day. My recipe for homemade soup takes at least three hours.

**A:** So now you don't have to start from scratch. You can just pop the top of a Manischewitz broth and use it to create your favorite dishes.

**Q:** Totally. I actually buy Manischewitz broth by the case. Having it on hand helps me get a quick jump on soups, stews, and lots of other dishes. It's an ingredient in nearly 50 recipes in this book. I love having a pareve option too—your vegetable broth. I'm always finding new ways to use a soup as more than, well, soup.

**A:** A lot of people use them to add oomph to all sorts of dishes that you might not expect—pasta, potatoes, stuffing, veggies—and, of course, gravies and sauces. Try using a broth instead of water when you cook rice. It gives it so much flavor.

**Q:** I do that! And I may never go back to plain water again. Beside the convenience, I have another reason for preferring the new Manischewitz broths: My family's health.

**A:** That's an aspect of cooking that has taken center stage in recent years, and I'm glad to tell you that we've kept up with the times. Today, many people insist on foods that are free of artificial flavors, colors, or preservatives. That's why our broths are made from all natural ingredients and contain no MSG. We also have a low-sodium option for people watching their sodium intake.

**Q:** Another aspect of health is freshness. How long will Manischewitz broth stay fresh after it's opened?

**A:** Up to four days, in the refrigerator. But in most households it's eaten up before that.

**Q:** I know. I usually open multiple cartons at a time. What else should a home cook know about using these broths? Is there anything that could possibly go wrong?

**A:** They're just about foolproof. We've been creating kosher foods for over 120 years and we know that home cooks want wholesome taste and quality that's easy to prepare. Our new ready-to-serve soups are simply the latest in our evolving chain of products that combine convenience with tradition.

**Q:** Even my grandmother would approve.

**A:** I'm glad.

# {Not Your Standard Glossary!}

Note to my super-loyal readers: I know that you've probably memorized the Hebrew/Yiddish Glossary from my first *Quick & Kosher* book, so I apologize now for using some of the same definitions in this book. *Nu*\*—these words have been in use for thousands of years—why should their meanings change?

### Baalas Teshuvah (Hebrew)

One who was not raised Orthodox but who explored Jewish religion and culture, and as a result took on religious observance. This is the feminine construction of the term. A male would be referred to as a *Baal Teshuvah*. There are so many people who are BTs today that it has become a vibrant sub-culture of Orthodoxy.

### Balabusta (Yiddish)

The perfect homemaker: She cooks, she cleans, she bakes, she owns the best spice rack. And she does it all with grace, donating her spare time to local charities.

### Bubbie (Yiddish)

Nanny, Grammy, Grandma—the woman with the soft wrinkles and soft arms, candy in her pocket and a tissue up her sleeve, hugging you, and telling you everything will be okay.

### Chalav Stam (Hebrew)

Milk that was not supervised by a Jew during milking or processing. There are Jewish legal implications concerning *chalav stam* and *chalav Yisrael*—but don't ask me to go there. Ask your rabbi.

### Chalav Yisrael (Hebrew)

Milk that was supervised by a Jew; the cow doesn't know the difference, but we do.

### Chulent (Yiddish)

The slowest cooking beef and bean stew in existence. You start it before Shabbos and it simmers all night until it's served the next day. Its rich aroma fills the house. The Yiddish term comes from the French word for warm, "chaud," as *chulent* was developed as a means of putting piping hot food on the table in honor of Shabbos. Sephardic Jews call this dish *chamin*, which means the same thing.

### Chupah (Hebrew)

Marriage canopy—but so much more! From the day a Jewish child is born, the mother is anxiously looking forward to escorting him or her to the *chupah*. She's four years old and still wants her pacifier? No matter—she'll be rid of it by the time she gets to her *chupah*!

### Daven (Yiddish)

To pray. But the Yiddish word hints that you are accustomed to direct dialogue with G-d, and you know He's listening. When you pray, you just stand there—but when you *daven*, you sway, you sing, you cry, you negotiate.

**Erev Shabbos (Hebrew)**

Friday afternoon, when the hours fly by and you realize that you haven't baked the *kugel* yet, the kids refuse to take a bath, the sun is going down, and the chicken still looks too raw.

**Kitniyos (Hebrew)**

A category of foods not eaten by Ashkenazic Jews on Passover: It includes rice, corn, peas, mustard seed, and all beans—grains and vegetables that can be cooked or baked in a fashion similar to grains forbidden on Passover. The ban includes derivatives too, such as corn oil. Sephardic tradition allows *kitniyos*, which is so terribly confusing to many of us. The bottom line is that if you're invited for a meal to someone's house on Passover, you'd better be sure you're both on the same page regarding these traditions.

**Knaidlach (Yiddish)**

Matzoh balls, but once again the translation doesn't do it justice. When you eat *knaidlach*, you can taste the love that went into making them.

**Kugel (Yiddish)**

The essential Jewish carb. More like an English pudding than anything else, it can fill you for three days. It's a Shabbos classic, so some people have an insatiable addiction to it. It can be made of either potatoes or noodles, but now it has developed into a score of varieties, from apple *kugel* and pineapple *kugel* to vegetable *kugel*, to you-name-it *kugel*.

**Latkes (Yiddish)**

Potato pancakes fried in oil, customary on Chanukah, but so good you may add them to your repertoire year-round. The oil is a reminder of the rededication of the Holy Temple in Jerusalem in ancient times, when a small jar of oil meant to burn for one day in the Golden

Menorah miraculously lasted for eight days. With my recipe for *latkes*, they won't last more than eight minutes. They're usually eaten straight from the pan, with family and guests standing over you as you fry. You're lucky if you get them to the table.

**Mashgiach (Hebrew)**

A kashrus-knowledgeable person who supervises the processing or cooking of kosher food whether it's at a farm, a manufacturing plant, a restaurant, or hotel kitchen. A *mashgiach* must be alert and savvy and not prone to falling asleep on the job.

**Minyan (Hebrew)**

Literally, ten men gathered for prayer services. The term has come to mean the service itself, as in "I can't do that shopping for you now, I'm going to *minyan*."

**Mitzvah (Hebrew)**

Not a "good deed," as popularly thought. We're not Boy Scouts going for Merit Badges. A *mitzvah* is an action mandated by G-d and carried out by us for the express purpose of doing His will. If G-d made it a *mitzvah* to eat heartily before Yom Kippur, who are we to argue? Other interesting *mitzvos* include buying your wife jewelry before a holiday, lighting Chanukah candles, buying your wife jewelry before a holiday, donating charity, buying your wife jewelry before a holiday, honoring your parents, and buying your wife jewelry before a holiday.

**\*Nu (Yiddish)**

There's no translation for *nu*, because the English language simply doesn't have the ironic depth to handle it. Closest thing to it is the French, *eh?*—and that's a poor second. If you don't understand *nu*, it won't kill you, but it might mean you've strayed too far from your Bubbie's chicken soup. *Nu*, what can you do about it?

## Shabbos (Hebrew)

The day to disconnect from your workday chores, worries, and mundane activities. It's the day to recharge spiritual batteries through praying, studying *Torah*, napping, and of course, eating well. A great family experience.

## Sheva Brachos [week] (Hebrew)

The first week of marriage—when fantasy and reality meet. You discover that your beloved can't stand your favorite toothpaste. You spend seven days running around to elaborate parties that are called "*Sheva Brachos*" because the "seven blessings" said under the *chupah* are repeated for the bride and groom during the Grace after Meals. After the third or fourth lavish *Sheva Brachos* banquet, you can no longer button your gorgeous bridal outfits and you go to the remaining ones in last year's *Shabbos* suit.

## Shidduchim (Hebrew, plural)

Suitable marriage partners. Parents, friends, and relatives of a marriageable individual are always on the lookout for a *shidduch*. Many a hopeful phone call starts with the exclamation, "Have I got a *shidduch* for your daughter!..." Sooner or later, the *shidduch* is a success and the parents can finally march her triumphantly to the *chupah*. (See above.)

## Shtetl (Yiddish)

A really small village in Eastern Europe. If you blink when you ride by, you'll miss it. Since most *shtetlach* were destroyed during the Holocaust, the word has come to mean any Jewish enclave where religious Jews go about their lives. It's a warm, homey place, where everybody knows everybody.

## Sukkah (Hebrew)

A temporary structure your husband puts up in the backyard with a lot of grunting and wheezing, so your family can live there—eating (and/or sleeping, depending on the climate) for the holiday of Sukkos. The "roof" is made of natural materials—branches or trendy bamboo—and is intentionally porous so the sunlight and rain can penetrate. Your job is to stay out of the way, and don't mention the little doo-hickey he forgot to attach.

## Torah (Hebrew)

Literally, the Five Books of Moses written on the parchment scroll you see in the synagogue. Commonly, the term embodies the Oral Law and all other sacred texts derived from it. The laws and statutes of the *Torah* are what make the Jewish people Jewish, with our unique lifestyle and values. The amazing thing about the *Torah* is that its multiple layers of meaning make it accessible and enlightening to everyone from age 3 to 120. There is no stronger bond between generations than studying *Torah* and living by its precepts.

## Yom Tov (Hebrew)

Literally a "Good Day," a generic term for Jewish holidays. It's a time to pull out all the stops on your menu.

## Yuntif (Yiddishization of Yom Tov)

Old-World slang used even by people whose only Yiddish consists of naming the parts of a chicken. For centuries, Jews have been greeting each other in the street (whether or not they're actually acquainted) during a Jewish festival with a smile and a nod and a "*Gut Yuntif!*"

# {Many Thanks}

They say it takes a village to raise a child; and to create a book, as well.
A large team of very talented and dedicated people are responsible for
making me, and this book, look good. Thanks to each and every one of
you for all your efforts on my part, for treating this book as if it were
your own, for believing in me, and for helping me to realize my dreams:

Yitzchak Feldheim, Mendy Feldheim, Eli Meir Hollander, and Feldheim
Publishers; Chesky Kauftheil, Aaron Dobrinsky, Devorah Goldman, and
Kosher.com; Charlotte Friedland; Julie Farkas; Sheilah Kaufman;
Paula Jacobson; Ann Stratton, Carrie Purcell and Pamela Duncan Silver;
Paige McCurdy-Flynn; Carol Winer; Ilya Welfeld, Shira Kallus, and Seymour PR;
Jay Buchsbaum and Gary Landsman; Fran Bar-Eli, Brigitte Mizrahi, Gil Oren,
Moshe Vogel, Elliot Budd, and Anderson International Foods; David Yale,
David Rossi, and The Manischewitz Company; Jay M. Eidelman, Debra Wells
and New Prospect Consulting.

I will be forever thankful to my mother, father, family and friends whose
everlasting physical and emotional support brought me to this day.

Mostly I would like to thank *Hashem*, because all *brachos* ultimately
come from Him.

# {Notes}

# {Notes}